Dizzy, busy AND Baking WITH A DIFFERENCE

By Nicky Cain

Copyright © 2023 Nicky Cain.

All rights reserved. No part of this publication may be reproduced, distributed, or transmitted in any form or by any means, including photocopying, recording, or other electronic or mechanical methods, without the prior written permission of the publisher, except in the case of brief quotations embodied in critical reviews and certain other noncommercial uses permitted by copyright law.

CONTENTS

A little bit about dizzy me 4

How I baked myself to a better me 5

Store Cupboard Essentials 6

A Note on Oven Baking 10

Freezing 10

Top Tips for keeping your
kitchen organised 24

Top 10 Tips for the Perfect Picnic 34

TREATS 11
Perfect Brownies 12

Milk Chocolate Brownies 13

Biscoff Blondies....................................14

Kinder Bueno Blondies........................15

Milky Bar Rice Krispie Bakes 16

Oven baked Chocolate Doughnuts 17

Oreo Cheesecake.................................18

Galaxy Bar Rice Krispie Bakes.............19

Biscoff Cheesecake..............................20

Brookies 22

Cadbury's Freddo Choc
Chip Cookies 23

CAKES 25
Victoria Sponge 26

Bakewell Cake 28

Gin and Tonic Cake 29

Chocolate Cake 30

Sticky Toffee Fudge Cake....................31

Lemon Drizzle Cake.............................32

Black Forest Gateau 33

SAVOURIES................35
Pizza Bombs 36

Pepperoni, Cheese and
Bacon-filled Tiger Loaf.......................37

Quiche Lorraine 38

Steak Pie 39	Birthday Chocolate Lollipops..............58
Full Breakfast Pie..................................40	Terry's Chocolate Orange Ice-cream 59
Lasagne Dome 41	
Parma Ham Arancini Balls...................42	Sweet Burger and Chips......................60
Halloumi Fries.......................................43	Rose Cupcake Bouquet........................62

AFTERNOON TEA 44

Bacon and Cheese Muffins 46	Red Velvet Cookies 63
Finger Sandwiches for Afternoon Tea.......................................47	Creme Egg Loaf 64
	Mini Egg Chocolate Cake 65
Plain Scones..48	Mini Egg topped Meringues................66
Cheese Scones 49	Sticky Toffee Apple Cake 67
Kinder Loaf Cake..................................50	Milk Choc Cinder Toffee.......................68
Bakewell Tart...52	Smores Brownies 69
Dairy Milk Fudge 53	Christmas Tree Mince Pie....................70

OCCASIONS 54

Birthday Brownie Cake 56	Christmas Gingerbread Cake 71
Brownie Chocolate Doughnuts 57	Christmas Fruit Cake 72

3

A LITTLE BIT ABOUT DIZZY ME

We are all busy parents, cooking, cleaning, working and looking after the kids, so this book is designed to be simple: straightforward recipes that are fun with easy-to-follow step-by-step methods.

This book is different. No long-winded recipes with 100 steps so you switch off when you get to step 3 and try to find an easier one to bake. My recipes are designed to be suitable for all stages of bakers, from beginners to people who have been baking for years.

My children love to get involved as much as they can when I am baking. They adore trying out any new recipes – yep, those sticky little fingers do somehow get into that bowl full of goodness every time – so this book is nice and simple for your children too. Your young ones can help you as you follow the recipes – and there's nothing better than the delicious result of a family bake.

I offer customers with food intolerances and allergies an option for most of my bakes and sweet treats when possible. It's no different in this book. You will find food intolerance sections for dairy free, and gluten free so anyone who suffers with allergies won't be missing out.

There's nothing more frustrating than having to get a long list of ingredients to make one cake – most of which you never use again! Each recipe has a section listing alternative ingredients that you can use. Us busy parents don't want to be dashing out for that one item, especially when you can use alternatives! The only exceptions are my recipes in the Occasions section. Sometimes, you just have to buy a few special ingredients!

Decoration is key. That finished look of the bake is just as important as the taste. But don't worry, I am not going to make you do anything complicated! All of my bakes are finished off with a simple-to-make ganache or buttercream – easy but at the same time a beautiful finish to your bake.

Along with opening my own baking business, it truly has been a dream come true to finally be typing my recipes to share with you, sipping my cup of tea whilst my dog, Buster, is beside me. And yes, I hear the word Mummy 50 plus times an hour too!

I hope you have as much fun as I do baking all my treats and savoury items. I had so much fun creating this book for you.

Nicky X

HOW I BAKED MYSELF TO A BETTER ME

I've had a passion for baking since I had kids and have always loved baking with them. My baking started off as a hobby. Then I introduced my baking to my two children, who loved getting involved with me.

For me, baking is theraputic and has helped me with anxiety and my mental health, which has been a big part of my life since I was 16. When I had my son, I struggled mentally with OCD cleaning. Now, instead of cleaning the floor 10 times a day, I make brownies instead! 😊😊

I currently juggle my baking obsession with my part time work for a bank as a new customer specialist. In fact, my hobby became a business.

My business was born two years ago, producing brownies and blondies. Since then, it has expanded and I now have a large menu, including savoury items and an ever increasing list of treats. I also produce afternoon teas to your door which has also expanded to graze platters too, large buffets and brunch afternoon teas. I started my afternoon teas as there was nobody else doing something like that locally. This service went off like you wouldn't believe purely from word of mouth and sharing posts on social media.

I can't thank my fabulous customers enough for purchasing my treats and continuing to follow my journey on social media. The support they have given me over the last two years has meant everything.

However, I can never stay still. I love nothing more than researching new products. Once I've completed making all the bakes for my customers, I regularly sit with a cup of tea to investigate creating my new treat or bake.

My little baking room is at the back of the house, where I create a lot of my treats whilst listening to good old Radio 1. The days fly by when I'm in my happy place.

STORE CUPBOARD ESSENTIALS

This book is all about making life easier for you when baking treats for you and your family to feast on, but at the same time no expensive costs are involved when buying the equipment needed for each recipe. However, there are just a couple of equipment essentials that will make your life easier. Don't despair if you haven't got them as I have looked at alternatives for you to use too.

THOSE USEFUL LITTLE GADGETS

You don't need a fully equipped kitchen for my recipes, but there is some equipment that you will need.

Baking Tin

The best size to get would be 9 inch x 9 inch or 8 inch x 12 inch. A standard baking tin from your local supermarket will absolutely be fine. It doesn't need to be an expensive known brand. Maybe share with a friend or relative – one buys one size and the other buys the second tin. (You just need to plan who is baking what and when!)

Loose-bottom Round Cake Tins

All my recipes are based on 8 inch (20cm) spring form, loose bottom cake tins. You can pick these up easily and cheaply either on-line or from all major supermarkets. Lots of my recipes need two of them, but they are inexpensive so it is worth it – more cake!

Loaf Tin

Just a standard loaf tin will be fine, either silicone or aluminium.

Ovenproof oval baking tin

This is for my lasagne dome. However, any ovenprove dish will work for this recipe – or even a deep square baking tray.

Tart Tin

There are a couple of recipes that you will need to use a tart tin. Ideally use a springform tin that easily loosens the base, making it easier to serve.

Cupcake tin

For cupcake recipes, ideally a 12-hole cupcake tin. Some of the recipes don't need you to use all 12 holes, in which case I have said so.

6-hole doughnut pan

You can get these from most homeware shops and online. But you could change the doughnut recipes into cupcakes and just use the cupcake tin instead.

Cupcake cases

These are so cheap to buy and help make things pretty. There's so much choice out there and you can match it with your colour scheme. But if you are pushed and don't have any in, two squares of greaseproof paper will do the job for you.

Whisk
Whisking can be a very physically demanding operation, especially if you are baking regularly. I would strongly recommend any baking enthusiast invests in an electric mixer. There are many available that all do exactly the same thing. They vary on price and this is usually dependant on how powerful they are. I would recommend one that is at least 300W – 450W.

Bowl
Any large ceramic, stainless steel, plastic or glass bowl will be fine. Glass and ceramic bowls can chip or break easily, simply by catching them on other plates and bowls when getting them out for use. These should be inspected closely for signs of damage before every use. My recommendation to save cost is to invest in stainless steel or plastic. There are many bowl sets that come with lids, which are really useful for the storage of mixed ingredients.

Rolling Pin
The ideal rolling pin needs to be a cylinder rather than tapered. As the standard pie tray is 7 inches in diameter, the pin needs to have at least 6 inches of flat rolling surface. A rolling pin is also very useful for crushing biscuits in a bag. For basic rolling tasks, a wine bottle could actually do the same job! (Any excuse to buy more wine for yourself! ☺)

Spoons
Spoons are must have items for every amateur and professional baker. Whether it's to help measure out ingredients, spoon mixtures into tins, or folding in flour. Along with the usual teaspoons, tablespoons and the trusty wooden spoon, a large metal spoon is essential for creating airy and soft sponge batter mix.

Sieve
A sieve is a cheap but very important piece of equipment for every baker. Sifting flour into your batter mix is essential for ensuring a fluffy, soft bake.

Scales or Electronic Scales
A key element to successful baking is precision. Ingredients must be measured out accurately to ensure a good quality bake. Scales come in many shapes and styles with both electronic and traditional 'gauge' type readily available. I find the electronic type are usually slim and much easier to clean and store than bulkier traditional style scale. Scales do not have to be expensive and I would not expect anyone to have to pay any more than £15 - £20 for a decent set of scales. Provided that they are well looked after and cleaned after every use, they should last a very long time.

Standard Chocolate moulds
Websites such as ebay or Amazon have plenty of styles and at those lovely affordable prices that we like! ☺

Cheap Stand Mixer
Not an essential as hand whisks could be used, but when making sponge batter, or whisking cream, this makes the process much quicker and may save your arms!

Measuring Jug
It's a handy thing to have in your kitchen anyway and again, you can get them cheaply. As well as measuring liquid, you can use them to heat things in the microwave (as long as it is a microwavable jug!).

Blind Baking Beans
Essential for blind baking pie and tart bases. Using rice is an alternative solution, but baking beans can be used over and over again.

Greaseproof Paper
As an alternative, you could just line the tin with butter.

Hand Mixer
A cheap hand mixer will be fine.

Airtight Container
Most of these bakes won't last long enough for you to need to store them as they will be gobbled up as soon as you put them on the table. However, if you have some left over that you need to store, it is worth having an airtight container or two. I would recommend some bowls with lids for creams, custards and sauces and also some Tupperware containers for cakes and brownies, etc.

INGREDIENTS

I try to make all my recipes as easy and straightforward for you as possible. This means making the best use of a few ingredients that will come in handy in your cupboard. However, I have suggested alternatives if you don't have the specific product in, plus I have made some recipes less expensive by using alternative products too.

These are the ingredients that should be in every store cupboard and fridge so that you will never be short on baking options!

Cupboard

Baking powder
Caster sugar
Flour – plain and self-raising
Golden syrup
Vanilla extract
Almond extract
Glacé cherries
Medjool dates
Flaked almonds

Whilst being a much-used ingredient, almonds come in bags, so once opened they will not last as long as almond extract. However, you can have some ready for decoration if you wish, by keeping them in the freezer for up to 18 months!

Dark chocolate
Always go for supermarket's own brand because it does the job just as good.

Cocoa powder
But not absolutely an essential item as you can always use dark chocolate.

Fridge

Butter
Whilst butter is usually stored in the fridge, most recipes call for either softened or melted butter. (Can be salted or unsalted. I have tried lots of recipes with either and I don't think it makes any real difference to the flavour of the bake.)

Eggs
I always have 6 large eggs in the fridge just in case I get the urge to bake some brownies.

Milk
Milk is not routinely required for most bakes but can be useful to moisten sponge batter if it mixes a little dry. Most households always have milk in the fridge, so it's there if needed.

A NOTE ON OVEN BAKING

For best results in your bakes, always ensure the oven is pre-heated to the desired temperature and the bake is placed in the centre of the oven. As you get to know your oven, you may notice that it is a bit uneven in the baking, so you'll just have to turn things around midway through the bake.

All my recipes have the temperature for regular oven Celsius (°C) and fan oven (°C). As a quick rule of thumb, when cooking in an electric fan oven, you'll need to reduce the Celsius temperature by 20°C.

TEMPERATURE CONVERSIONS

Gas Mark	Celsius (°C)	Fan (°C)	Fahrenheit (°F)
1	140	120	275
2	150	130	300
3	160	140	325
4	180	160	350
5	190	170	375
6	200	180	400
7	220	200	425

FREEZING

When it comes to freezing baking products, the options are a little restricted. No sweet bakes with creams, buttercreams and fondants can be frozen for storage.

Sponge cake layers can be made and frozen for up to three months. It is essential that the cake layers are fully baked and then allowed to completely cool. Once cooled, the layers must be individually wrapped and sealed with cling film before placing in the freezer. If they are flavoured sponges, it is a good idea to label the sponge before freezing.

A lot of the savoury bakes in this book can be frozen. Pies, quiches, flans and savoury muffins are really good for long term storage in the freezer, but again these must be allowed to fully cool and be individually wrapped before freezing.

TREATS

Everyone deserves a sweet treat now and again. The secret to the best treats is quick and simple recipes that all the family loves time and time again. Recipes that don't need anything extra apart from what you already have in the cupboard when the urge hits you or on a rainy day when baking together will be the only thing to stop the children from running wild!

Traybake recipes such as Brownies and Blondies are my family's favourites and these types of simple delicious bakes were the ones that convinced me to start my baking business. My traybakes continue to be hugely popular with my wonderful customers who love to personalise their Brownies with their favourite chocolate bars and biscuits.

Cheesecakes are also a firm favourite in my home and I have some simple recipes that guarantee trouble-free results and taste.

TREATS

PERFECT BROWNIES

There are two schools of thought when it comes to the perfect Brownie: cakey and crumbly, or denser and gooey. Whilst there is some middle ground on this, most of my customers and all of my family fall firmly into the denser and gooey camp. Although I always encourage using something from the cupboard, it is important that plain flour is not substituted for self-raising flour as this will encourage a rise in the bake and ultimately a cakier texture. The most crucial difference between the two is cooking time, plus it won't give you that gooey texture like plain flour does.

How to tell if your Brownies are done
To bake fudgy or gooey brownies you should bake them for around 25 - 30 minutes. This will ensure that the eggs are cooked whilst keeping the centre soft and dense. To get a more crumbly or 'cakier' brownie bake for at least another 5 minutes and repeatedly carry out the toothpick test until the centre of the bake is showing as clear on the toothpick.

Other than timings, there are two other ways of checking the brownies are done.

Visual check – After 25 minutes of baking, open the oven door and look at the surface of the brownie. It should have changed from a shiny dark surface to a matt and light brown finish. There should also be slight cracking on the surface.

Toothpick test – Insert a toothpick into the bake, both at the edge and in the centre. When you take it out from the edge it should come out dry and clear. When it is withdrawn from the centre it should come out with a smear of chocolate on it.

Once you have perfected your preferred baking times and consistency, you can start to add different types of your favourite chocolate bars to personalise the brownie.

With my brownie recipes you can generally adapt the recipe and add any types of chocolates that you want. Keep it nice and simple by using the same recipe but fill each brownie bake with whatever favourite chocolates you want. The great thing about brownies is you can eat them as they are or warm them up with a nice dollop of ice cream or cream. They are lovely to have any time of the year too, so yep, a good recipe all round!

TREATS

MILK CHOCOLATE BROWNIES

Makes 18 pieces

**Preperation time
20 minutes**
Bake time 25 minutes
Cool time 1 hour
Last 6 days at room temperature

You'll need:

Large mixing bowl
Heatproof bowl
Large metal spoon
Scales
8 inch x 8 inch baking tin
Greaseproof paper

TIP: Basically, you can use any of your favourite chocolates in this recipe and use a favourite brownie recipe. If you're anything like me – I love anything covered in Cadbury chocolate – why not use lots of different chocolate. A favourite is Ferrero Rocher and a pack of 16 is perfect. Instead of using Dairy Milk chocolate, push Ferrero Rocher chocolates into the brownie mixture when it's in the tin. Don't forget to keep some to put on the top!

INGREDIENTS

1 bar of 95 g Dairy Milk **chocolate**
150 g caster sugar
200 g dark chocolate
115 g butter (salted or **unsalted**)
3 small eggs
50 g cocoa powder
70 g flour
50 g white chocolate

INSTRUCTIONS

1. Preheat the oven to 180°C/160°C fan and line a baking tin with greaseproof paper.

2. Melt together 100g of the dark chocolate and butter in a heatproof dish in the microwave for about 1 minute and then set aside to cool.

3. Using an electric whisk or spoon whisk the eggs with the caster sugar until light and fluffy.

4. Pour the chocolate and butter mixture into the caster sugar and eggs and give it a good stir and make sure everything's incorporated together.

5. Sift the flour and cocoa powder into the brownie mixture and give it a good stir. Make sure you don't over mix as you don't want to knock any air out of the brownie mixture but make sure everything's mixed together. Pour your bake in the prepared tin then add in the Dairy Milk chunks.

6. Bake in the oven for approximately 25 minutes. Make sure you don't over bake as you want that slightly gooey mixture in the inside but still making sure it's cooked.

7. Optional: Melt the rest of the dark chocolate in the microwave and spread it on to your baked brownie. Melt the white chocolate in a separate heatproof dish and spread swirls of the white chocolate on top of the brownie base.

TREATS

BISCOFF BLONDIES

Well what can I say? Biscoff, Biscoff, Biscoff! ☺ This has got to be one of my top sellers in my sweet treats menu, and my personal favourite. You can practically use Biscoff in almost any dessert, but I think it goes extremely well in a blondie bake, especially both the spread and biscuits, and I promise you that you will not be disappointed.

Makes 18 pieces
Preparation time 20 minutes
Bake time 30-35 minutes
Cool time 1 hour

You'll need:
Large mixing bowl
Heatproof bowl
Large metal spoon
Scales
12 inch x 8 inch baking tin
Greaseproof paper

INGREDIENTS

350 g plain flour
280 g caster sugar
170 g melted butter (salted or unsalted)
Jar of Biscoff spread
Half a pack of Biscoff biscuits
100 g white chocolate chunks
2 small eggs

INSTRUCTIONS

1. Preheat the oven to 180°C/160°C fan and line a rectangular tin with greaseproof paper.

2. Beat the caster sugar and eggs in a large bowl until nice and smooth then add the melted butter. Beat again until all the mixture is incorporated together.

3. Add the plain flour to your mixture and give it a good mix until it forms a batter mixture.

4. Pour half the mixture into your tin and swirl approximately 5 spoonfuls of Biscoff spread into the blondie mixture. Place about 8 Biscoff biscuits in between each swirl of Biscoff spread.

5. Add the rest of the blondie mixture. Place in the oven and bake for approximately 30-35 minutes until there is an ever-so-slight wobble in the middle.

6. Melt the white chocolate in a microwave safe bowl and drizzle across the top of your blondie. Put another 8 Biscoff biscuits on top of your bake. Leave to cool fully before cutting into squares.

TREATS

KINDER BUENO BLONDIES

Kinder Bueno is such a favourite treat in my household and one of my preferred chocolate bars to use in my bakes. You can choose this lovely treat in most bakes and with that lush hazelnut cream-filled chocolate bar with small amounts of wafer filling, it is a popular treat for both adults and kids. I use it in cheesecakes, brownies, and cakes but I think my most popular Kinder Bueno dessert is this ultimate BLONDIE! ☺

Makes 18 pieces
Preparation time 20 mins
Bake time 30-35 mins
Cool time 1 hour

You'll need:
Large mixing bowl
Heatproof bowl
Large metal spoon
Scales
12 inch x 8 inch baking tin
Greaseproof paper

Tip: An alternative recipe which is a favourite of mine is the Jammie Dodger blondie. After you have poured half the mixture into your tin, place a pack of Jammie Dodgers on top with a couple of spoonfuls of raspberry jam. Then pour the rest of the blondie mixture on top. Once cooked and cooled slightly, add another pack of Jammie Dodgers on top with 100g melted chocolate swirled over the biscuits.

INGREDIENTS

350 g plain flour
280 g caster sugar
170 g melted butter (salted or unsalted)
Pack of Kinder Bueno chocolate bars
200 g white chocolate chunks
2 small eggs

INSTRUCTIONS

1. Preheat the oven to 180°C/160°C fan and line a rectangular tin with greaseproof paper.

2. Beat the caster sugar and eggs in a large bowl until nice and smooth, then add the melted butter. Beat again until all the mixture is incorporated together.

3. Add the plain flour to your mixture and give it a good mix until it forms a lovely batter mixture.

4. Pour half the mixture into your tin and place half the packet of Kinder Bueno pieces evenly over the blondie mixture. Then place 100 g of the white chocolate chunks between the Kinder Bueno pieces.

5. Add the rest of the blondie mixture then put in the oven and bake for approximately 30-35 minutes until there is an ever-so-slight wobble in the middle.

6. Melt the white chocolate in a microwave safe bowl then swirl on top of your blondie.

7. Finally, after allowing the bake to cool for around 1 hour, add the rest of the Kinder Bueno chunks on top.

TREATS

MILKY BAR RICE KRISPIE BAKES

These little treats are so quick and easy to make and as an added bonus, there is no baking involved! It is such a lovely treat for your kids to get involved with too. I remember when I was a child and Rice Krispies were the go-to for most bakes. I have such wonderful memories tucking into Rice Krispie treats at my friends' parties – yum! There are so many different chocolates that you can add to this recipe. Milky Bar is just one of them and who doesn't love Milky Bar white chocolate! ☺

Makes 6 large pieces

Preparation time
20 mins

Bake time No baking involved

Refrigeration time
3 Hours

Would recommend storing them in an airtight container so they could be enjoyed for up to 7 days.

You'll need:
Large mixing bowl
Heatproof bowl
Large metal spoon
Scales
9 inch x 9 inch baking tin
Greaseproof paper

INGREDIENTS

140 g butter

260 g Rice Krispies

300 g marshmallows

1 bar of 85 g Milky Bar chocolate

200 g white chocolate

TIP: You can easily substitute the Milky Bar chocolate for any other preferred chocolate such as milk chocolate, even using store's own brand chocolate.

INSTRUCTIONS

1. Grease and line a 9 x 9 inch baking tin with greaseproof paper.
2. Melt the butter and marshmallows in a heatproof dish in the microwave for about 30 seconds. Once melted, add the Rice Krispies and give them a good stir so everything is incorporated.
3. Pour the mixture into the tin and spread it out evenly so the base is covered.
4. Add half of the Milky Bar chunks evenly over the mixture
5. Melt the white chocolate chunks in a microwave safe dish then pour over the mixture and Milky Bar chunks. Spread it so that everything is covered.
6. Add the rest of the Milky Bar chunks evenly on top then put the tin in the fridge for about 3 hours until the chocolate is firm.
7. Portion the tray up into 6 large chunks or smaller if you prefer.

TREATS

OVEN BAKED CHOCOLATE DOUGHNUTS

Is there anything better than a yummy chocolate-covered doughnut? These doughnuts are so easy to do and are a winner in my household, both with my kids and my husband – they absolutely love them! And my kids love making them too. These doughnuts can be dipped in any of your fave chocolates, but I find that milk and white chocolate is the ultimate. And you can add any of your fave chocolates on top! Plus, believe it or not, there is the bonus of cutting down on the calories because they have fewer calories than fried doughnuts – so any excuse to have another one! ☺

Makes 6 large doughnuts

Preparation time 20 minutes
Bake time 25 minutes
Cool time 20 minutes
Setting Time 1 Hour
Will comfortably stay fresh for at least 5 days if stored in an airtight container.

You'll need:

Large mixing bowl
Heatproof bowl
Large metal spoon
Scales
6-hole doughnut pan (you can get these from most homeware shops and online)

INGREDIENTS

120 g self raising flour
70 g caster sugar
30 g melted butter
1 egg
100 ml semi skimmed or full fat milk
100 g of milk or white chocolate chunks

TIP: You could also add choc chips to the recipe, or after you have baked the doughnuts, let them cool and add a sprinkle of icing sugar to each doughnut instead of melted chocolate.

INSTRUCTIONS

1. Preheat the oven to 180°C/160°C fan.
2. In a large bowl, whisk the eggs and caster sugar then add your melted butter till everything is incorporated together.
3. Sift the flour into your wet mixture and give another good stir until no flour bits remain, but try not to overmix the batter.
4. Finally add the milk and give another good stir. You now have your doughnut batter!
5. Spoon the batter into the doughnut tin. I use a measuring jug for this as it's easy to pour in each doughnut cavity.
6. Place the doughnut pan in the oven and cook for approximately 20-25 minutes.
7. Remove from the oven and let them cool in the pan for about 20 minutes.
8. Melt your favourite milk or white chocolate topping in a microwave safe dish then dip each doughnut in the melted chocolate and put on a plate to set, adding any of your favourite chocolate piece toppings.

17

TREATS

OREO CHEESECAKE

I prefer no-bake cheesecakes so much more to baked ones as I find they are creamier and are so much easier to make. ☺ And who doesn't like Oreos? You will find that you can easily adapt my cheesecakes to any of you favourite chocolate toppings too, whatever your or your family's favourites are, such as Kinder, Galaxy or Maltesers.

Serves minimum of 8 people

Preparation time 20 mins
Bake time No baking involved
Refrigeration time 3 Hours
Will comfortably stay fresh for at least 5 days if stored in an airtight container.

You'll need:

Large mixing bowl
Heatproof bowl
Large metal spoon
Scales
8 inch round cake tin
Greaseproof paper

INGREDIENTS

300 g Oreo biscuits
125 g melted butter
300 g cream cheese
3 tablespoons of caster sugar
400 ml double cream
2 packs of Oreos

INSTRUCTIONS

1. Blitz the biscuits in a food processor to a fine crumb, then mix in the melted butter and press the mixture firmly into an 8 inch spring form tin.

TIP: If you don't have a food processor, then simply put the biscuits into a bag and give them a pound with a rolling pin until crushed to the desired consistency.

2. With a hand mixer, mix the cream and sugar together until it's thick and holds itself. If you can tip the bowl over and the contents don't not start to fall then it's thick enough! Add the cream cheese and beat the mixture together. Fold 1 pack of the crushed Oreos into the cream cheese filling.

3. Spread the mixture evenly over the biscuit base then top with the other pack of Oreo biscuits crushed over the top.

4. Leave to set in the fridge for approximately 3 hours.

TIP: You could add 100g melted milk chocolate to the cream cheese mixture before adding on top of a Digestive biscuit base.

TREATS

GALAXY BAR RICE KRISPIE BAKES

Now who doesn't Like Galaxy chocolate? I think I could go through a large bar of it in no time at all! ☺ Again, the kids will love getting involved with this recipe and it is so easy.

Makes 6 large pieces
Preparation time 20 minutes
Bake time No baking involved
Refrigeration time 3 hours
Store in an airtight container for 5 days

You'll need:
Large mixing bowl
Heatproof bowl
Large metal spoon
Scales
9 inch x 9 inch baking tin
Greaseproof paper

INGREDIENTS

140 g butter
260g Rice Krispies
300 g marshmallows
1 large Galaxy bar
200 g milk chocolate

Tip: Be careful to use exactly the right amount of butter for this recipe because if you go a little bit over it won't set. Also, get it in the fridge as soon as possible to set.

INSTRUCTIONS

1. Grease and line a 9 x 9 inch baking tin with greaseproof paper.
2. Melt the butter and marshmallows in a heatproof dish in the microwave for about 30 seconds. Once melted, add your Rice Krispies and give a good stir so everything is incorporated.
3. Pour your mixture into a tin and spread out evenly so all the sides are covered.
4. Add half the Galaxy bar chunks evenly over the mixture.
5. Melt the milk chocolate chunks in a safe heatproof dish and pour over the mixture and Galaxy bar chunks. Spread the melted chocolate so everything is covered.
6. Optional: Add the rest of the Galaxy bar chunks evenly on top and set in the fridge for about 3 hours until the chocolate is firm.
7. Portion up into 6 large chunks or smaller if you prefer.

TIP: You can use a Milky Bar (or any white chocolate) instead of Galaxy for a white chocolate treat

TREATS

BISCOFF CHEESECAKE

TREATS

This cheesecake is one of my most popular cheesecakes. The combination of Biscoff and cheesecake is the ultimate dessert. A delicious no-bake cheesecake with a buttery biscuit base then a Biscoff creamy cheesecake filling topped with Biscoff crumbs, this is one for the Biscoff lovers.

Serves minimum of 8 people
Preparation time 20 mins
Bake time No baking involved
Refrigeration time 3 hours
Can be stored in a fridge for at least 3 days

You'll need:
Large mixing bowl
Heatproof bowl
Large metal spoon
Scales
8 inch round cake tin
Greaseproof paper

INGREDIENTS

300 g digestive biscuits
125 g unsalted melted butter
300 g cream cheese
3 tablespoons of caster sugar
400 ml double cream
Half a tub of Biscoff spread
4 Biscoff biscuits

Tip: You could put the rest of the Biscoff spread on the cheesecake before you add your crushed biscuit topping. Just warm it slightly and pour over the chilled cheesecake (and maybe add a couple of extra whole biscuits on the top too!)

INSTRUCTIONS

1. Blitz the digestive biscuits into a fine crumb in a food processor, then mix in the melted butter and press firmly into an 8 inch spring form tin. If a food processor is not available, simply put the biscuits into a clean food bag and crush with a rolling pin. This can be quite therapeutic!

2. With a hand mixer, mix the cream and sugar together until it's thick and holds itself. Add the cream cheese and beat the mixture together. Fold in the Biscoff spread.

3. Spread the mixture evenly over the biscuit base then top with crushed Biscoff biscuits.

4. Let set in the fridge for approximately 3 hours.

TREATS

BROOKIES

You may not have heard of these yummy treats. They are a mix between a cookie and brownie and are absolutely delicious. These have been a big seller to my lovely customers as you are combining the best of both worlds of a yummy gooey brownie with a chocolate chip cookie. Yep, the best combination and such an easy recipe to make and turns out so chewy, rich and chocolatey.

Makes 18 pieces
Preparation time 20 minutes
Bake time 30-35 minutes
Cool time 1 hour
Store in an airtight container for 5 days.

You'll need:
Large mixing bowl
Heatproof bowl
Large metal spoon
Scales
12 inch x 8 inch baking tin
Greaseproof paper

INGREDIENTS

Brownie
150 g caster sugar
200 g dark chocolate
115 g butter (salted or unsalted)
3 small eggs
50 g cocoa powder
70 g plain flour

Cookie
115 g melted butter
1 egg
150 g caster sugar
150 g flour
1 bag of chocolate chips

TIP: Best to have a couple of bowls ready when preparing this bake for the cookie mixture and the brownie.

INSTRUCTIONS

1. Preheat the oven to 180°C/160°C fan and line a baking tin with greaseproof paper.

2. Melt together 100 g of the dark chocolate and butter in a heatproof dish in the microwave for about 1 minute and then set aside to cool.

3. Using an electric whisk or spoon, whisk the eggs with the caster sugar until light and fluffy.

4. Pour the chocolate and butter mixture into the caster sugar and eggs and give a good stir. Make sure everything's incorporated. Sift the flour and cocoa powder into the brownie mixture and give a good stir. Make sure you don't overmix as you don't want to knock any air out of the brownie mixture but make sure everything's mixed together. Put your gooey brownie mixture into a baking tin whilst you make your cookie dough.

5. For the cookie batter, add the caster sugar and eggs into a large bowl and add the melted butter. Give it a good stir to make sure everything's incorporated.

6. Sift in the flour and add the chocolate chips then give the mixture a good stir. Swirl spoonfuls of your cookie batter into the brownie mixture evenly until you have used up all your cookie mixture.

7. Bake in the oven for approximately 30-35 minutes until an inserted knife comes out clean.

8. Once baked, let cool on the side for about an hour then cut into 18 pieces.

TREATS

CADBURY'S FREDDO CHOC CHIP COOKIES

The classic chocolate chip cookie with the delicious gift of a Cadbury's Freddo. These cookies are absolutely yummy. I have tried loads of different styles of cookies and these are simply the best – chunky and with that lovely soft centre but crunchy outer layer. Cadbury's Freddos are one of my favourite chocolates of all time, but to be honest, anything to do with Cadbury is alright by me! These Freddos are just right size for these yummy cookies. Kids will love to make these with you and they are a lovely after dinner treat.

Makes 6 large cookies

Preparation time 20 minutes

Bake time 25 minutes

Cool time 1 hour

Can be stored in your traditional biscuit tin, or an airtight container for 5 days.

You'll need:

Large mixing bowl

Heatproof bowl

Large metal spoon

Scales

9 inch x 9 inch baking tin

Greaseproof paper

INGREDIENTS

200 g flour

115 g melted butter

150 g caster sugar

100 g pack of chocolate chips

1 small egg

Six pack of chocolate Freddos

Tip: For the topping of these cookies you can use any of your favourite chocolates. A favourite with my customers has got to be Kinder chocolates, and you can even add a Nutella or Biscoff topping. ☺

INSTRUCTIONS

1. Preheat the oven to 180°C/160°C fan and line a baking tin with greaseproof paper.

2. Mix together the caster sugar and egg until everything is incorporated, then pour in the melted butter and give a good stir again.

3. Sift the flour into the wet mixture and give another good stir until you get a cookie dough mixture, then add the chocolate chips and give another final stir.

4. Place 6 large spoonfuls of the cookie mixture onto the tin and cook for approximately 25 minutes.

5. Once cooked, let cool for about 10 minutes and then place your chocolate Freddos on top. (so that they don't melt but stick to the top of the cookie)

TOP TIPS FOR KEEPING YOUR KITCHEN ORGANISED

1. Throw away any unwanted or unneeded items and always check the expiry dates.
2. Give your cabinets a good clean regularly. (I set out some time every year, before I stock up with all my Christmas goodies.)
3. Have set cupboards for certain items so a cupboard for all your pots and pans, a cupboard for all your cleaning products, etc.
4. Make sure you have a kitchen system that suits you and that things are put nearest where you usually use them. e.g put your cups and saucers next to your kettle, your bread near your toaster.
5. Organise your food so that frequently used items are stored at eye level. Where possible, keep the same sorts of items together, e.g canned foods and spices placed in one part of the cupboard.
6. Keep all leftover chocolate or treats in a separate container ready to use for your next bake. If you are anything like me and my kids, we do tend to tuck into this little treat box when we have used up everything in our treat cupboard!

CAKES

You can't beat a good old Victoria sponge classic cake, that fluffy cake that the whole family can feast their eyes on before tucking in. With my sponge cake recipe, you can adapt it in so many ways, by adding different chocolates, fruit and even cocoa powder. That basic recipe turns from a vanilla sponge to a chocolate sponge just like that – easy!

You can use my cake recipes for any special occasion or just as a nice Sunday dessert after that family Sunday roast.

When filling and decorating cakes there are so many options to go for – e.g buttercream, whipped cream or jam. All of my cake recipes have a plain, simple and easy buttercream but feel free to experiment when you get the knack!

CAKES

VICTORIA SPONGE

The Victoria sponge cake is a two-tier light and fluffy cake filled with buttercream and jam and topped with fresh strawberries. Also known as Victorian sandwich or Victoria Cake and considered as one of the most popular tea time treats. This is one of my very first cakes that I prepared, which was for an afternoon tea, and since then I think I have baked dozens and dozens for afternoon teas and general celebration cakes.

You can adapt this recipe by substituting the strawberry jam for any other of your favourite jams, curds and fruits, or use whipped cream as an alternative to buttercream (like in the picture).

Serves 12

Preparation time 15 minutes
Baking time 40 minutes
Cool time 1 hour
Keeps in an airtight container for 4-5 days

You'll need:

Large mixing bowl
Heatproof bowl
Large metal spoon
Scales
Two 8 inch round baking tins
Greaseproof paper

TIP: Use the wrapper that the butter comes in to grease the tin so you don't get your hands all greasy.

CAKES

INGREDIENTS

400 g butter
400 g caster sugar
400 g self raising flour
7 eggs
3 tablespoons of strawberry jam
200 g pack of strawberries

Buttercream
200 g butter
400 g icing sugar

PREPARATION

Good preparation is crucial to getting soft, fluffy sponges. Having all the ingredients measured out in advance will speed up the batter making process which will reduce the time available for the batter to lose the incorporated air.

The butter must be as soft as possible without starting to melt. This will allow the butter to bond easier with the sugar, causing more air bubbles during the beating process.

Make sure the eggs are as fresh as possible and that they are at room temperature. Fresh, room temperature eggs will hold more air than older, straight from the fridge eggs. If you store eggs in the fridge, I would recommend taking them out the night before.

INSTRUCTIONS

1. Heat your oven to 180°C /160°C fan.
2. Butter two 8 inch (20 cm) sandwich tins and line with greaseproof paper.
3. In a large bowl beat together the caster sugar and butter in your stand mixer and then add the eggs one at a time. Beat thoroughly before adding the next egg. This will ensure the mix does not get too wet and dense.
4. Finally, sift the flour into the mix and fold gently with a large metal spoon until you have a smooth soft batter. To check the consistency of the batter, use the large metal spoon and check the mixture drops easily from the spoon. Be careful not to repeat this test too many times as it will encourage the air to escape from the batter mix.
5. Divide the mixture equally into two round baking tins then level and smooth with a teaspoon.
6. Place in the centre of the pre-heated oven and cook for 20 - 25 minutes, until golden. To check the sponges are cooked, press the sponge slightly and check that it springs back. As a final check, insert a thin metal skewer into the middle of the cake and it should come out clean.
7. Turn out both sponges onto a cooling rack with the bottoms facing upwards and leave to one side until completely cool.
8. To make the buttercream, beat the butter and icing sugar until smooth and creamy and spread evenly, about 1 cm thick, onto the bottom of one of the sponges. Then spread a 1cm thick even layer of the jam to the bottom of the other sponge and carefully sandwich both sponges together to form the sandwich cake.
9. Finish off by dusting the top of the cake with icing sugar and decorating with strawberries on top.

CAKES

BAKEWELL CAKE

Anything Bakewell is my utmost favourite; I absolutely love anything with that almond taste. Whenever my family and I go out for a meal, the first thing I look out for on the desert menu is, yes you got it, BAKEWELL! ☺

I bake lots of Bakewell treats, from blondies and brownies traybakes to Bakewell tarts and even Bakewell cookies. I am just completely in love with Bakewell. ☺ This yummy cake has an almond sponge and is filled with a vanilla buttercream and jam. To finish off the Bakewell look, I sprinkle lots of flaked almonds on the top. I have never actually been to Bakewell but that's definitely my aim, so that I can try out all their delicious treats.

Serves 12

Preparation time 15 minutes
Baking time 25 minutes
Cool time 1 hour
Keeps in an airtight container for 4-5 days

You'll need:
Large mixing bowl
Heatproof bowl
Large metal spoon
Scales
Two 8 inch round baking tins
Greaseproof paper

INGREDIENTS

400 g butter
400 g caster sugar
400 g self raising flour
7 eggs
2 teaspoons of ground almonds
100 g flaked almonds
3 tablespoons of strawberry jam

Buttercream
200 g butter
400 g icing sugar

INSTRUCTIONS

1. Preheat your oven to 180°C/160°C fan and line two cake tins with greaseproof paper. Rub a little butter on the paper so it sticks inside each tin.

2. Beat the butter and sugar until light and fluffy then add the eggs one at a time and beat again until everything's incorporated.

3. Sift the flour and add the ground almonds then fold with a large metal spoon gently until you get a nice smooth, almond filled batter.

4. Split the mixture into the two tins and bake in the centre of a pre-heated oven for 20 – 25 minutes.

5. Let the cakes cool on one side for about an hour whilst you make your buttercream.

6. Beat together the butter and icing sugar until you form a smooth paste. Spread half of the buttercream on the top side of the first sponge and the jam on the top side of the other and then gently sandwich both cakes together. Spread the rest of the buttercream on top. (Alternatively, you can mix some icing sugar and water together and top the cake with icing – as I have in the picture.)

7. Finish off the cake by sprinkling with flaked almonds.

Tip: You could halve the base ingredients and make cupcakes instead. Using the butter, caster sugar, eggs and flour mixture, fill 8 cupcake cases halfway, then add a teaspoon of raspberry jam. Then fill with the rest of the sponge mixture. Bake in the oven for the same amount of time then add your buttercream on top. Finish with the flaked almonds and a cherry on each cupcake.

CAKES

GIN AND TONIC CAKE

My Gin and Tonic cakes have always been a favourite with the adults. So popular for a birthday treat or for that special summer's picnic. I mean, what goes nicer with a glass of gin and tonic than a nice slice of Gin and Tonic cake – plus it's an absolute showstopper! This cake is infused with gin and tonic drizzle which makes it even more light and airy. The sponge is so soft and the cake looks absolutely delightful with the mini gin bottle set into the buttercream on top of the cake.

Serves 12
Preparation time 15 minutes
Baking time 25 minutes
Cool time 1 hour
Keeps in an airtight container for 4-5 days

You'll need:
Large mixing bowl
Heatproof bowl
Large metal spoon
Scales
Two 8 inch round baking tins
Greaseproof paper

INGREDIENTS
400 g butter
400 g caster sugar
400 g self raising flour
7 eggs

Drizzle
100 g caster sugar
A splash of gin
A splash of tonic water

Buttercream
200 g butter
400 g icing sugar
1 lime

Tip: If you don't like alcohol, you can substitute for non-alcoholic gin. There are so many good non-alcoholic gins available now to choose from and they taste equally as good.

INSTRUCTIONS

1. Preheat your oven to 180°C/160°C fan and butter and line the bases of two 8 inch (20cm) round cake tins with greaseproof paper.

2. Firstly, make the gin and tonic drizzle to pour on your sponges once they are baked. Measure out the ingredients and place everything into a pan. Put your pan on the hob on a very low heat and give it a good stir. Heat gently for approximately 5 minutes until the liquid starts to bubble slightly and reduce to a consistency similar to thin custard. The drizzle will not harden as it cools, so it is ok to leave it to one side whilst your prepare your cake batter.

3. Beat the butter and caster sugar with an electric mixer until light and fluffy and then add the eggs one at a time until the mixture is combined. Then sift in the self raising flour and fold gently until everything is incorporated together.

4. Split the cake mix evenly between the two tins and level out gently with the back of a spoon. Bake the cakes for approximately 25 minutes. Let the cakes cool in the tin for about 10-15 minutes, then place onto a plate whilst you make your buttercream.

5. To make the buttercream, beat the butter on its own for a couple of minutes until smooth then add the icing sugar and beat again until completely combined and fluffy.

6. Place the buttercream on top of the first sponge, then add the second sponge on top and spread over the remaining buttercream.

7. Place your mini gin bottle on top of cake and decorate with a thinly sliced lime.

TIP: There are so many different flavoured gins as well as many infused or flavoured tonics. Any favourites would work equally as well, so feel free to experiment.

CAKES

CHOCOLATE CAKE

This is my favourite homemade chocolate cake, with a super moist sponge and with that lovely chocolate flavour. Who doesn't like a slice of chocolate cake? This recipe can be used for a celebration cake – just add your favourite chocolates on top – or simply as a lovely desert to have any time of the year. But one thing I can guarantee you is that it will definitely be a crowd-pleaser.

Serves 12

Preparation time 15 minutes
Baking time 40 minutes
Cool time 1 hour
Keeps in an airtight container for 4-5 days

You'll need:

Large mixing bowl
Heatproof bowl
Large metal spoon
Scales
Two 8 inch round baking tins
Greaseproof paper

INGREDIENTS

400 g butter
400 g caster sugar
400 g self raising flour
7 eggs
30 g cocoa powder

Buttercream
200 g butter
400 g icing sugar
60 g cocoa powder

TIP: You could also use of your favourite sprinkles – sugar coated or chocolate sprinkles – or even your favourite chocolate chunks as a topping.

INSTRUCTIONS

1. Heat your oven to 180°C / 160°C fan and butter two sandwich tins and line with greaseproof paper.

2. In a large bowl beat together the caster sugar and eggs and then add the butter until everything's incorporated together, then follow with your flour and cocoa powder and give another good mix.

3. Divide the mixture in to the two tins then smooth with a teaspoon and place in the oven. Cook for 40 minutes. You will know when the cake is cooked when you insert a knife in the middle of the cake and it comes out clean.

4. Leave the cake to one side until completely cool.

5. To make the buttercream, beat the butter, icing sugar and cocoa powder until smooth and creamy. Spread on one side of the cake, and then sandwich both cakes together.

6. Spread the rest of the buttercream thinly and evenly on top of the cake. For best results, I would recommend using a spatula with a good flat surface and taking some time to get an even spread.

CAKES

STICKY TOFFEE FUDGE CAKE

The Sticky Toffee Fudge Cake is a rich, fudgy, amazingly yummy cake. It will get those taste buds going, and is my husband's all-time favourite desert. This cake is absolutely beautiful served still warm and is a great cake to have on those cold nights when you're snuggled by the fire.

Serves 12
Preparation time 15 minutes
Baking time 40 minutes
Cool time 1 hour
Keeps in an airtight container for 4-5 days

You'll need:
Large mixing bowl
Heatproof bowl
Large metal spoon
Scales
Two 8 inch round baking tins
Greaseproof paper

INGREDIENTS

250 g Medjool dates
180 ml boiling water
125 g butter
225 g dark brown sugar
4 eggs
250 g self raising flour
125 g black treacle

Buttercream
200 g butter
400 g icing sugar

Decoration
Fudge pieces

INSTRUCTIONS

1. Preheat the oven to 180°C/160°C fan and line two baking tins with greaseproof paper.

2. Chop the dates up into squares of about 2cm, then pop them into a bowl and add the hot water. Leave to soak for about 10 minutes.

3. Put the sugar and eggs into a mixer and blend together, then add the butter and flour and give another good mix until smooth. Add the black treacle and the soaked dates and beat again.

4. Pour the mixture into the two tins and bake for approximately 40 minutes until a knife inserted comes out clean. Once baked leave to cool on the side whilst you make your buttercream.

5. Beat the butter and icing sugar together until a thick cream forms. Once the cakes have cooled, spread a 10mm layer of buttercream onto one side of one of the sponge cakes and sandwich both of them together. Use the rest of the buttercream for the top of the cake.

6. Finish the cake by scattering some fudge chunks over the top.

Tip: Why not try it warm with a dollop of cream or your favourite ice cream? Yum!

CAKES

LEMON DRIZZLE CAKE

This cake is certainly a film favourite in most households for sure and is fabulous any time of the year In the summer with a glass of lemonade or in the cold months with a dollop of custard. You can't beat the zingy lemon taste and that lovely moistness of the sponge.

Serves 12

Preparation time 15 minutes

Baking time 40 minutes

Cool time 1 hour

Keeps in an airtight container for 4-5 days

You'll need:

Large mixing bowl

Heatproof bowl

Large metal spoon

Scales

Two 8 inch round baking tins

Greaseproof paper

INGREDIENTS

400 g butter

400 g caster sugar

400 g self raising flour

7 eggs

2 tablespoons of lemon extract

1 lemon

Buttercream

200 g butter

400 g icing sugar

1 tablespoon of lemon extract

INSTRUCTIONS

1. Heat your oven to 180°C / 160°C fan and butter two sandwich tins and line with greaseproof paper.

2. In a large bowl beat together the caster sugar and eggs and then add the butter until everything's incorporated together, then follow with the flour and the lemon extract then give another good mix.

3. Divide the mixture in to the two tins then smooth with a teaspoon and place in the oven and cook for 40 minutes. You know when the cake is cooked when you can insert a knife in the middle of the cake and it comes out clean.

4. Leave the cake to one side until completely cool.

5. To make the buttercream, beat the butter and icing sugar until smooth and creamy and then add the lemon extract. Spread on one side of the cake, then add the jam to the other cake and then sandwich both cakes together.

6. Then finish off by placing your thinly sliced lemons on top or drizzle some of the icing over the cake.

CAKES

BLACK FOREST GATEAU

A delicious two-layer chocolate sponge cake with cherries and more chocolate. One of my favourite deserts of all time and such a classic old school cake. I have adapted my black forest gateau and made yummy gooey brownies, which has also been a crowd-pleaser on my menu. The black forest gateau is fabulous for any celebration or lovely for a weekend treat after a Sunday roast.

Serves 12
Preparation time 15 minutes
Baking time 40 minutes
Cool time 1 hour
Keeps in an airtight container for 4-5 days

You'll need:

Large mixing bowl
Heatproof bowl
Large metal spoon
Scales
Two 8 inch round baking tins
Greaseproof paper

INGREDIENTS

400 g butter
400 g caster sugar
400 g self raising flour
7 eggs
3 tablespoons of black cherry jam
25 g cocoa powder
Tin of 'Pie filling' black cherries

Buttercream
200 g butter
400 g icing sugar

Decoration
Fresh cherries
Dark chocolate sprinkles

Tip: You can also turn this recipe into mini cupcakes too by using half of the ingredients for the sponge cake and adding a spoonful of blackcurrant jam in the centre of each sponge. Use the buttercream for the topping and add a cherry and sprinkles to finish.

INSTRUCTIONS

1. Heat your oven to 190°C / 170°C fan and butter two sandwich tins and line with greaseproof paper.

2. In a large bowl, beat together your caster sugar and eggs then add your butter until everything's incorporated. Follow with your flour, cocoa powder and give another good mix. Finally add your tin of black cherries (including the sauce from the tin too) and give another good final stir.

3. Divide the mixture into two tins, place in the oven and cook for 40 minutes. You will know when the cake is cooked as when you insert a knife in the middle it comes out clean.

4. Leave the cake to one side until completely cool.

5. To make the buttercream, beat the butter and icing sugar until smooth and creamy and then spread on one side of the cake, and then spread the blackcurrant jam on the other side and then sandwich both cakes together.

6. Finish off by adding the rest of the buttercream on top of the sandwiched cake and top with fresh black cherries and the chocolate sprinkles (or chunks of chocolate and a bit of edible glitter for that special occasion).

TOP 10 TIPS FOR THE PERFECT PICNIC

1. Freeze grapes or any of your favourite fresh fruit. They are a great snack in the heat — and healthy too! You could even pop them in your drink as ice.
2. Messy sandwiches that fall apart are never quite as appetising as when they were first made, so why not try using some string to tie them together so they stay closed until you are ready to eat them.
3. Why not try a nice fresh salad rather than sandwiches, or a pasta salad that everyone can share.
4. For sun safety, make sure you pack all your sun creams, sunhats and sunglasses for yourself and little ones.
5. Whether it's a Frisbee, ball or teddy bear, don't forget to bring a few games to entertain you all.
6. Make sure you check the weather the night before or that morning to see whether you need to pack any essentials: umbrella, raincoat, etc.
7. Always have a spare plastic bag to put all your rubbish in.
8. Prepare your goodies ahead and keep them in the fridge for an hour to keep them cooler longer.
9. Try not to go overboard so you are carrying most of it back again.
10. Try to use any cans or bottles from the fridge so they will stay cooler for longer.

SAVOURIES

I am a big fan of all things savoury. If you asked me to choose between a dessert and a starter when I go out for a meal, it would be a starter every time. This chapter is just some of my favourite savoury treats, from my yummy Arancini balls (a delicious Italian dish with risotto and Parma ham), to my fresh-filled tiger loaf – now that's a treat for the whole family to tuck into on a Saturday night! I bake a lot of my savoury treats in my prepared buffets for weddings, and other celebration events, plus in my afternoon teas too. My pie recipes are packed with flavour and great to prepare ahead at the weekend, then you are able to freeze them and defrost for a tasty mid-week meal.

SAVOURIES

PIZZA BOMBS

Pizza has been hailed the world's best takeaway so here is my spin on this classic. My Pizza Bombs are a great fun recipe to do with the kids or simply an easy recipe to do through the week for all the family to tuck into, using shop bought dough with all your favourite toppings. I bake these savoury treats as part of my buffet package, and they are also perfect for children's parties, as long as they have been left long enough to cool before serving to children. This appetiser is perfectly gooey and has bursts of flavour, enriched with pepperoni and mozzarella and finished off with Italian herbs. Yummy! ☺

Serves 4
Preparation time 15 minutes
Baking time 20 minutes
Best served fresh from the oven
These can be kept in the fridge for 2 days covered

You'll need:
12-hole muffin tray

Tip: You could use various fillings for this recipe. So instead of pepperoni, you could use mushrooms or sundried tomatoes for a veggie option with mozzarella.

INGREDIENTS
Olive oil
1 shop-bought pizza dough
Supermarket's own tomato pasta sauce
Mozzarella ball cut into 8 slices
16 slices of pepperoni
1 tablespoon of dried Italian herbs

INSTRUCTIONS
1. Preheat your oven to 180°C /160°C fan.
2. Brush each muffin hole with a little oil and divide the pizza dough into 8 portions. Roll each portion into little balls, then use your fingers to flatten and stretch into a 3-4 inch round, or about the diameter of a standard coffee mug.
3. Place half a teaspoon of the tomato sauce on the dough then top with a slice of mozzarella followed by 2 pieces of pepperoni.
4. Fold the edges of the dough up and around the filling, then twist to seal the contents inside. Place one of the filled dough balls in each muffin hole and scatter half a teaspoon of the dried Italian herbs over each pizza bomb.
5. Bake in the oven for approximately 20 minutes until golden brown. Once cooked, remove from the oven and let them cool down before serving.

SAVOURIES

PEPPERONI, CHEESE AND BACON-FILLED TIGER LOAF

Tiger loaves have got to be my favourite bread of all time; that crunchy topping gives a beautiful textural contrast to the soft inside. It's called a tiger loaf because the first baker who made it thought it looked striped like a tiger. You can fill your loaf with any of your favourite savoury treats, but I personally find these three ingredients are such a wonderful combination – like a pizza but with chunky bread. Heaven on a plate, don't you think? This is one of my most popular savoury treats, especially at the weekends, and my customers definitely return to order more! ☺

Serves 4
Preparation time 20 minutes
Baking time 5 minutes
Best served straight from the oven
Once cooled, keep covered with tinfoil and best eaten within 24 hours

You'll need:
9 inch x 9 inch baking tin
Greaseproof paper

Tip: For a vegetarian version, you could simply use onion, or tinned tuna, and follow the same method.

INGREDIENTS

1 large tiger loaf
Pack of cubed bacon (salted or unsalted)
125 g grated cheese
20 slices of pepperoni

INSTRUCTIONS

1. Heat your oven to 190°C /170°C fan.

2. Line a baking tin with greaseproof paper and bake the diced bacon for approximately 10 minutes until just cooked through.

3. Whilst the bacon is in the oven, slice your tiger loaf in a criss-cross shape about a third of the depth without cutting through to the bottom. Pull away every other diamond shape of bread so you can start to fill with your tasty treats.

   Tip: You could use the leftover croutons for any homemade soups that you do. Simply place in a sandwich bag and freeze them for whenever needed.

4. Once the bacon is cooked and slightly cooled, fill evenly inside the bread, followed with the cheese and pepperoni. Once you have used up all your ingredients, pop the filled loaf back into the oven for about 5 minutes until the cheese has melted.

SAVOURIES

QUICHE LORRAINE

This mouth-watering dish is probably one of the best-known French dishes. It can be served as a starter with a crisp salad on the side or as an evening meal with a side of new potatoes or chips – depending on how naughty you want to be! (Personally, chips all the way for me! ☺) It can also be served warm or cold. My quiches are served in a lot of my afternoon teas. There are many variations and flavours so you can also adapt this recipe really easily by using the standard egg and cream cheese base and adding diced onion and grated cheese for a comforting cheese and onion quiche. This recipe is so easy to make. You can also experiment further with things like broccoli, salmon or even leftovers such as chicken that you may have in the fridge for great, flavoursome alternatives to the standard cheese quiche. The kids can help you too!

Serves 6

Preparation time 15 minutes
Baking time 30 minutes
Can be eating straight from the oven or chilled
Store covered in the fridge for 2 days

You'll need:
Large mixing bowl
Large metal spoon
Scales
9 inch x 9 inch baking tin
Foil

Tip: Why make things complicated for yourself when you can buy already made shop-bought pastry tart cases?

INGREDIENTS

Readymade savoury tart pastry case
3 medium eggs
125 g grated mature cheddar cheese
300 g soft cheese
Salt and pepper for seasoning
80 g smoked cubed bacon

INSTRUCTIONS

1. Preheat your oven to 180°C /160°C fan.
2. Line a baking tin with tin foil and cook the bacon according to packet instructions then set aside.
3. Whisk the eggs in a measuring jug (or if you don't have one of these, a deep bowl will do) then add the cream cheese and a pinch of salt and pepper, and give a good stir.
4. Place the pastry case on the baking tin. Scatter the cooked bacon and grated cheese over the pastry case then pour in the cream cheese evenly till it fills just below the pastry top.
5. Bake in the oven for about 25 minutes then remove and leave to cool.

SAVOURIES

STEAK PIE

When it's cold outside, there is nothing more comforting than a delicious warm pie. This steak pie has everything you need in a comfort food pie. Tasty homecooked strips of beef in a rich beef gravy. Even better, it's super easy to make and will feed the whole family. You could even make this and freeze once cooled to enjoy its comforting taste another day. This is great for a Sunday lunch served with a side of vegetables or make ahead and warm up on a busy week day with some chips on the side. I make my steak pie with a shortcrust pastry but you can also make it with puff pastry if that is what you prefer – of have in the fridge in a readymade pack! Whichever is your preference, both are yummy! ☺

Serves 4
Preparation time 20 minutes
Baking time 40 minutes
Best served straight from the oven
Once cooled keep covered in the fridge for up to 2 days , or alternatively, once cooled, freeze or up to 3 months in the freezer.

You'll need:
Frying pan
Large metal spoon
8 inch round baking tin
Greaseproof paper
Measuring jug

INGREDIENTS

2 packs of shortcrust pastry
500 g quick frying beef strips
2 white onions
2 beef stock cubes
1 egg
2 tablespoons of flour
Salt and pepper for seasoning
1 tablespoon of vegetable oil

INSTRUCTIONS

1. Preheat your oven to 160°C /140°C fan.
2. Grease an 8 inch cake tin with a little bit of butter. Roll out your first pastry sheet and place the pastry inside the cake tin, making sure all sides and the base are covered. Trim off any excess pastry you have that is overhanging in the tin.
3. Heat the oil in a large frying pan and add the beef. Cook for about 5-10 minutes until it's browned all over.
4. Add the chopped onions and cook for a further 5 minutes until they start to soften.
5. Add the flour and seasoning and give a final good stir.
6. Finally add 600ml of boiling water to your beef stock cubes and pour the mixture into the pan with the beef. Cook on a low heat for about 10-15 minutes until the sauce starts to thicken.
7. Spoon everything into the pastry-lined tin then roll out your second pastry sheet and smooth over the top of the pie. Cut off any hanging excess, then crimp the edges, using you thumb and forefinger, so it's fully sealed, making two small slits in the pie lid to allow heat to escape during the cooking.
8. Beat the egg in a small bowl using a fork. Finish the pie by brushing the top with the beaten egg wash using your fingers or a pastry brush (if you have one) then put in the oven and bake for approximately 30-35 minutes until the pastry is crisp and golden.

TIP: You can also use chicken and chicken stock instead of beef, and add cooked vegetables to the pie. Part boil any vegetables for 5 minutes and drain, prior to baking.

SAVOURIES

FULL BREAKFAST PIE

These large puff pastry pies are definitely a comfort food pleaser and can be eating any time of the day. What better way for a full breakfast lover to enjoy the full breakfast meal in one bite, surrounded with a yummy puff pastry? Sometimes you just need comfort food, whatever the time of year it is! ☺ This pie is so easy to make and a fun way to use puff pastry for breakfast. It's a classic flavour combination and you can change the recipe to your liking. You could add ingredients such as black pudding or mushrooms. For vegetarians, using veggie sausages and bacon. Yum, and with a dollop of brown sauce or ketchup at the side, where can you go wrong? ☺

Serves 6

Preparation time 30 minutes

Baking time 40 minutes

Can be eaten either hot or cold

This can be stored in the fridge covered for 2 days

You'll need:

Large mixing bowl

Large metal spoon

8 inch round cake tin

Greaseproof paper

INGREDIENTS

2 packs of ready made puff pastry

8 rashers of smoked bacon

8 supermarket own sausages

12 frozen hash browns

1 tin of baked beans

1 egg

Tip: You could put baked beans in the middle layer if you like to keep it moist. You could even put your favourite red or brown sauce inside – my favourite is brown sauce every time!

INSTRUCTIONS

1. Firstly, add your bacon, sausage and hash browns to a baking tin and cook them according to the packet instructions, then leave to the side covered in foil.
2. Heat your oven to 160°C /140°C.
3. Roll out your puff pastry and grease an 8 inch cake tin with a little butter. Fill the inside of the tin with the pastry so that it covers the whole of the inside and cut off any excess that is overlapping the tin.
4. Layer the inside with the bacon, sausages, hash browns and beans straight from the tin until you get to just below the top of the cake tin.
5. Roll out your second sheet of puff pastry and place it over the cake tin, then cut away the excess pastry. Gently pinch both pastry sheets together until the pie is completely closed.
6. Using a brush, brush the top of the pie with the egg yolk so it gives that glossy shine finish.
7. Bake in the oven for approximately 30-35 minutes until it starts to turn a lovely golden colour.

SAVOURIES

LASAGNE DOME

Lasagne has become a British classic and is fabulous served with a fresh, crisp salad or if you're feeling rather peckish, some yummy chunky chips. This lasagne dome recipe uses the same ingredients used in a normal lasagne, but it is basically shaped in a dome and looks wonderful in the centre of any table for everyone to tuck into. I love anything Italian and pasta is one of my favourite dishes so I could eat this at least once a week. You could also easily turn this recipe to be suitable for vegetarians by substituting the minced meat with spinach.

Serves 4

Preparation time 40 minutes
Baking time 25 minutes
Best served straight from the oven
Once cooled, keep covered in the fridge for up to 2 days. Or cover and freeze.

You'll need:
Large pan
Large metal spoon
Ovenproof oval baking tin

INGREDIENTS

3 teaspoons of vegetable oil
500 g minced beef
A pack of diced onions or 2 whole onions chopped
Jar of white béchamel sauce (such as Dolmio)
Pack of fresh lasagne sheets (about 12 sheets)
Tin of tomatoes
Garlic clove chopped
Teaspoon of black pepper and salt

INSTRUCTIONS

1. Heat your oven to 160°C /140°C fan.
2. Heat 2 tablespoons of vegetable oil in a large pot over high heat and add the mince beef. Cook until the meat starts to brown all over. Add the seasoning to the pot with the onions and garlic and give another good stir. Cook for another 5 minutes.
3. Add the tinned tomatoes, reduce the heat to medium and bring the sauce to a simmer, and cook it down until the sauce becomes thick (about 15 minutes).
4. Grease a large oven safe bowl with another tablespoon of vegetable oil and lay the lasagne sheets so they cover the whole inside of the bowl. The lasagne sheets should just hang over the sides at the top of the bowl.
5. Spread half of the meat mixture over the lasagne sheets, then layer another 3 sheets over the meat mixture, add the béchamel white sauce, and another 3 sheets of the lasagne then finishing off with the meat mixture.
6. Fold the lasagne sheets which overlap the edge of the bowl over the meat mixture and add the last of the lasagne sheets on the top. Cover with tin foil and bake in the oven for about 40 minutes.
7. To serve the lasagne, simply cut the dome into slices.

Tip: Use the same recipe and instead of shaping it into a dome, use a standard baking tin and prepare like a basic lasagne.

SAVOURIES

PARMA HAM ARANCINI BALLS

Arancini balls are an Italian dish and are often seen at artisian markets. Oh, how I love to visit a food market once in a while with my family and try out local produce. Yes, it's one of my favourite things to do when we have quality family time together. These Arancini balls are sticky balls of risotto rice filled with Parma ham and mozzarella then coated in fresh breadcrumbs. You can add your favourite fillings, but I find Parma ham and mozzarella are the best combination. But you can use anything you have or what's left over in your fridge. Lots of items work well together – normal ham, mushrooms or even cream cheese.

These Arancini balls are lovely as a starter with a crisp salad. I use them as part of my afternoon tea dishes and buffets. They are also great to make ahead if you are having an upcoming party. Freeze once cooled in the fridge and defrost them the night before. Warm them in the oven for about 5 minutes before serving.

Serves 4
Preparation time 40 minutes
Baking time 20 minutes
Best served straight from the oven
Once cooled, these can be covered and frozen

You'll need:

3 small bowls
Large metal spoon
Frying pan
Baking tin
Greaseproof paper

INGREDIENTS

15 g butter
300 g risotto rice
900 ml vegetable stock
1 ball of mozzarella
100 g flour
2 beaten eggs
200 g breadcrumbs
8 slices of Parma ham

INSTRUCTIONS

1. Heat 15g of butter in a large frying pan and add the risotto rice, then cook gently for about 5 minutes. Add the stock to the pan, stirring all the time until you have used up all your stock, then continue to cook for approximately 15 minutes. Once cooked through, set aside and leave to cool.

2. Once the risotto has cooled completely, shape into 8 large round balls, preferably egg shape size, and fill each ball by pushing a piece of mozzarella cheese and a piece of ham into the rice, then make sure they are completely covered with the rice.

3. Put the flour, eggs and breadcrumbs in three different bowls and coat the balls firstly with the flour then the egg and finally the breadcrumbs. Space them out on baking tin.

   TIP: If you want your balls extra crunchy, repeat the process with flour, egg and breadcrumbs.

4. Bake in the oven for approximately 10-15 minutes until the breadcrumbs start to turn a lovely golden colour.

   Tip: These can also be used as part of a tapas themed evening. I use these balls as part of my tapas afternoon tea and they go down a storm every time, alongside sliced meats and halloumi cheese, or pre-brought chicken skewers and a mix of olives.

SAVOURIES

HALLOUMI FRIES

This is such a popular treat, great for both kids and adults and perfect for any occasion, whether it a weekend treat or as a side dish with any meal. Plus there is literally only two ingredients so not an expensive recipe at all but such a popular dish and ready in minutes. These fries are a whole new level of goodness and the ultimate appetiser snack. ☺

Serves 2
Preparation time 10 minutes
Baking time 5 minutes
Best served straight from the fryer

You'll need:
Large mixing bowl
Frying pan

INGREDIENTS

250 g halloumi cheese
3 tablespoons of plain flour
1 teaspoon of paprika
Vegetable oil for frying

Tip: You can double up your ingredients if you are looking to serve these fries to more people. You can also add your favourite dipping sauce to dip your fries. Mine is mayonnaise every time, but sweet chilli dipping sauce is a favourite with these halloumi fries. ☺

INSTRUCTIONS

1. Cut your block of halloumi into 14 even pieces.
2. Mix your flour and paprika in a bowl then roll the fries in the mixture until they are fully coated.
3. Heat the oil in a large frying pan, then add the haloumi fries for a few minutes each side until they turn into a lovely golden colour. Remove from the pan and place on a plate.
4. Serve immediately.

A REALLY EASY DIP RECIPE:

1 garlic clove
1 red chilli
50 g caster sugar
3 tablespoons of white wine vinegar

Place all of your ingredients in a pan with a 100ml of water, bring to the boil and simmer for 3-5 minutes until the chilli has softened and the sauce has reduced by half. Take off the heat and pour into a dish to serve.

AFTERNOON TEA

The afternoon tea was introduced to Britain in the early 19th Century. At the time, it was usual for people to take only two meals a day: breakfast, and then dinner at around 8pm. It was said that ladies from the upper classes would take tea and a snack in the afternoon to stave off feelings of hunger before dinner. Before long, all fashionable society was sipping tea and nibbling sandwiches in the middle of the afternoon. Sadly, these days, afternoon tea is considered an occasional luxury for the British – a birthday treat, or special occasion.

An afternoon tea was traditionally composed of sandwiches (usually delicately cut into triangles or fingers), sweet pastries and cakes. Interestingly, although scones (with jam and clotted cream) are generally considered a main component of an afternoon tea, they were only introduced to the menu in the twentieth century.

I have been making my afternoon teas for the last two years and I can honestly say this is where my business took off. I have a variety of menus, both sweet and savoury, from delicious finger sandwiches to old fashioned scones, plus additional sweet treats and pastries, all washed down with Britain's favourite tea or even a cheeky glass of prosecco. Such a lovely thing to have with friends and family in the summer, sat on a picnic blanket or even a large family occasion.

In this chapter I have provided some simple treats that are the best part of an afternoon tea. Those lovely scones, both savoury and sweet, an assortment of cakes, and some of my savoury treats that have always gone down a storm!

There are no hard and fast rules when it comes to the menu. However, the key elements to any good afternoon tea are sandwiches, pastries, scones and, of course, a pot of tea. The sandwich fillings and types of treats should be tailored to your guests. Plan ahead by consulting your guests to make sure there is something for everyone.

There should always be a symmetry to the way the sandwiches are cut and presented. Small fingers or triangles with all bread crust removed is essential for nice, neat presentation.

Tiered cake stands are always the best way to show off your goodies. The food is best set out on the cake stand in a way that it is obvious to your guests, from where they are sat, which of the goodies are theirs. It's always fabulous if the table is set with a clean, crisp white tablecloth(or even a disposable table cloth), and the tiered food stands positioned so every guest can reach the stand without standing or stretching too far. If possible, serve clotted cream and jam separate from the scones; each guest should be given individual ramekins or small bowls.

Cutlery and china tea pots and cups are a must when it comes to serving tea, along with good china plates to eat from. This adds to the theatre of the afternoon tea and brings a formal and special feeling to the occasion.

Good stainless steel knives always look good. Silver cutlery is the perfect choice, and whilst these can be quite expensive, you can, with a bit of effort, pick these up quite cheap in charity shops, plus cake forks, and little spoons for the jam and cream. The same goes for the china. A mix of styles can look quirky and fun - perfect with a few posies of flowers dotted along the table.

TOP TIPS FOR THE BEST AFTERNOON TEA

1. Include light cakes, scones and sandwiches – always the top three treats for any afternoon tea!
2. Cute matching china isn't an essential but always gives that pretty afternoon tea feel – or even ask your guests to bring their own cup and saucer.
3. Any tea bags can be used for your afternoon tea: tea bags, pyramid tea bags or loose tea, but I always think it's nice to make a special effort and serve loose tea in a lovely glass jar or container - just don't forget the tea strainer!
4. Decorate your garden if you're having an afternoon tea on a lovely summer's day. Go wild with bunting or even pick some flowers from your garden and pop them in a vase or three, or even jam jars with ribbon.
5. Always cover your sandwiches with a clean tea towel or cloth to keep them fresh.

AFTEROON TEA

BACON AND CHEESE MUFFINS

These savoury muffins are really easy and once you have made them, you certainly won't want to go back to the store bought ones again. They are so tasty and an absolute must for any delicious afternoon tea. You can eat them warm or cold — however you like it. It is best to cook the bacon first as it brings out the flavour and gives you delicious crispy little chunks in every bite. Absolutely fine to be reheated for a few minutes in the oven, as they are delicious eaten warm with a smearing of butter, but are just as nice cold accompanied with some soft cheese and coleslaw. These muffins can also be rewarmed in a microwave for a couple of minutes.

Serves 8
Preparation time 15 minutes
Baking time 20 minutes
These will keep for 2-3 days in an airtight container

You'll need:
Large mixing bowl
Heatproof bowl
Large metal spoon
Scales
12-hole muffin tin
Muffin cases

INGREDIENTS

300 g self raising flour
80 g grated cheese
125 g melted butter
1 egg
250 g full fat milk
200 g diced bacon (ideally, cooked first in the oven)
Salt and pepper to season

INSTRUCTIONS

1. Preheat oven 180°C/160°C fan. Line a 12-hole muffin tin with paper muffin cases.

   Tip: If you do not have muffin cases, you can easily use two squares of greaseproof paper, overlapped to form a case in each cavity of the muffin tin.

2. Sift the flour into a large bowl then add the remaining ingredients.

3. Fold the mixture gently with a spoon so all the ingredients are distributed evenly.

4. Divide the mixture into the muffin cases and bake in the oven for approximately 20 minutes or until golden.

5. Allow to cool in the tin for 10 minutes before transferring them to a cooling rack or plate.

AFTEROON TEA

FINGER SANDWICHES FOR AFTERNOON TEA

FINGER SANDWICHES FOR AFTERNOON TEA

The 'first course' and the cornerstone of any afternoon tea is the sandwiches. Usually delicately cut into fingers or triangles. Now, I'm not going to tell you how to make a sandwich! However, all the sandwiches should be well presented and the same size, easy to handle and generally speaking be eaten in two or three bites.

SANDWICH FILLINGS

Whilst there are many recognised sandwich fillings (and you can choose your favourite), my most popular fillings are spring cheese (grated cheese, mayonnaise and spring onion), egg mayonaise, chicken and bacon, and tuna mayonnaise.

A usual standard size of afternoon tea consists of 4 fingers or triangles per person, but I do tend to double that for my customers so that they have a variety of flavours to choose from. After all, you can always keep them in the fridge and have a sneaky supper snack later!

AFTEROON TEA

PLAIN SCONES

There aren't any rules when it comes to what you have in an afternoon tea, but I would always recommend a crumbly, buttery scone every time – with clotted cream and jam or just a spread of butter. It's always the perfect accompaniment to sandwiches and they look amazing as part of the theatre of an afternoon tea. There are many variations to choose from, by adding mixed fruit or chocolate chips (see my alternative options at the bottom of the recipe) or simply this classic plain scone recipe.

Serves 8

Preparation time 15 minutes
Baking time 15-20 minutes
Store for 3-4 days in an airtight container

You'll need:

Large mixing bowl
Heatproof bowl
Large metal spoon
Scales
Baking tin
Greaseproof paper

Tip: Why Not try adding a cup of chocolate chips or mixed dried fruit. You can add these in after you have added the flour and use the same method and ingredients. It's as easy as that! ☺

INGREDIENTS

100 g melted butter
100 g caster sugar
500 g self raising flour
2 eggs
120 ml full fat milk

TIP: A brush of milk will do if you don't have enough eggs and you can even use your finger if you haven't got a brush.

INSTRUCTIONS

1. Pre-heat your oven to 200°C /180°C fan.
2. Mix the egg in a large bowl with a spoon, and then add the melted butter and make sure you give another good stir to make sure everything's incorporated.
3. Add in the flour and milk then start to knead the dough together until it starts to resemble breadcrumbs and the dough is no longer sticky.
4. Lightly flour your work surface and finish of kneading your dough for a good 5 minutes till it is soft and forms a neat ball.
5. Roll out your dough with a rolling pin until about 2 cm thick and then cut into 8 x 80mm dimeter discs, using a standard 80mm pastry or cookie cutting ring.
6. Line a baking dish with greaseproof paper and place your scones on top. Beat the second egg and brush on top of the scones.
7. Bake in the oven for 15-20 minutes or until golden.

AFTERNOON TEA

CHEESE SCONES

These cheese scones are the perfect afternoon tea delight, especially for the savoury lovers. They are light, fluffy and delicious and are best served warm with a spread of butter. You can even have these with a bowl of soup on a cold day.

Serves 8
Preparation time 15 minutes
Baking time 15-20 minutes
Will keep in an airtight container for 2 days

You'll need:
Large mixing bowl
Heatproof bowl
Large metal spoon
Scales
Baking tin
Greaseproof paper

INGREDIENTS

250 g self raising flour
60 g melted butter
125 g grated cheese
1 egg
160 ml full fat milk

Tip: You can use any type of grated cheese – mature, mild or extra mature – depending on what you prefer. I personally like a good mature cheddar, but other strong cheeses such as Red Leicester, Cheshire, or even Parmesan work well, the stronger the better, so you really get that tangy flavour in the scone. It's good to have a variation of sweet and savoury in your afternoon tea. Feel free to experiment with many different cheeses to find out which is your favourite.

INSTRUCTIONS

1. Preheat your oven to 200°C /180°C fan. Measure the flour into a bowl, and add the melted butter, then add the grated cheese and egg. Using your hands, mix it all together till you get a mixture resembling fine breadcrumbs.

2. Measure the milk in the jug then slowly add it in to your mixture until you have a soft but firm dough. Don't add it all at once as you want to make sure you get the right consistency.

3. Bring the dough together so it's nice and soft but not too sticky. If you find it has got a little too wet, just add a little bit more flour to your dough.

4. Lightly sprinkle flour to your work surface and roll out your dough until about 2 cm thick. Using a cookie cutter, cut out your scones and pop them onto a greaseproof baking tin.

5. Beat the egg in a small bowl using a fork. Brush the tops with a little egg wash using your fingers and bake them in the oven for 15-20 minutes.

AFTEROON TEA

KINDER LOAF CAKE

My kids absolutely love any recipes with Kinder chocolates in. This rich chocolate loaf cake is packed with Kinder chocolates and is absolutely delicious with an afternoon tea, especially for the chocolate lovers. Not only are the chocolates inside, but the cake is also topped with more chocolates and a rich chocolate buttercream – yummy! This loaf cake is so easy to make and slices into portions easily, ready for your guests.

Serves 10

Preparation time 15 minutes
Baking time 40 minutes
Will keep in an airtight container for 4 days

You'll need:

Large mixing bowl
Heatproof bowl
Large metal spoon
Scales
Loaf tin
Greaseproof paper

AFTEROON TEA

INGREDIENTS

Cake

225 g butter
225 g caster sugar
175 g self raising flour
50 g cocoa powder
3 eggs
120 g Kinder chocolate bars

Buttercream

120 g butter
250 g icing sugar
3 tablespoons of cocoa powder
Any Kinder products to decorate the top

INSTRUCTIONS

1. Preheat your oven to 180°C /160°C fan.
2. Using a small knob of butter, grease your loaf tin and line with greaseproof paper.
3. In a mixing bowl, cream the butter and sugar together then add the eggs. Give it a good stir until everything's incorporated.
4. Sift in the flour then cocoa powder and gently fold (slowly stir the ingredients) the mix together, using a large metal spoon. The key here is to retain as much air as possible to encourage the rise during baking, so slow and steady.
5. Add your Kinder chocolates and give another gentle fold. Pour the mixture into the loaf tin.
6. Place in the centre of the oven and bake for approximately 40 minutes. You can check the loaf is completely baked by inserting a metal skewer into the middle of the bake. If it comes out clean you know it is ready.
7. Once the loaf is ready, remove from the oven, turn out onto a cooling rack and leave to cool. The loaf can be eaten and enjoyed either warm or completely cool.
8. For the buttercream, cream the butter until fluffy with a large spoon, then add in your icing sugar and give another good stir until fully combined.
9. Add the cocoa powder and give the mixture another final stir. Then spread the buttercream on top of your baked loaf.
10. Finish off your bake by adding any Kinder chocolates you wish on top of the buttercream or you could even use any other chocolates you have in the house.

Tip: Turn this yummy recipe into cupcakes – an absolute treat for adults and kiddies! All you need to do is add 50g more of the flour. Half fill the cupcake cases with the cake mixture then add a piece of Kinder Bueno chocolate, then fill the rest of the cases before baking for the same amount of time as in the recipe.

AFTERNOON TEA

BAKEWELL TART

The yummy Bakewell tart is a classic British desert and a lovely family favourite. Served warm with thick cream or even custard, this tart is so versatile. The Bakewell tart is lovely to have in the summer for an afternoon tea picnic in the garden or on those cold days by the fire with your friends and family.

Serves 8

Preparation time 15 minutes

Baking time 20 minutes

Will keep in an airtight container for 2 days

You'll need:

Large mixing bowl

Heatproof bowl

Large metal spoon

Scales

Tart tin

Roll of ready-made shortcrust pastry

INGREDIENTS

150 g butter

150 g caster sugar

150 g self-raising flour

2 teaspoons of almond extract

3 eggs

3 large tablespoons of cherry jam

200 g icing sugar

50 g flaked almonds

Glacé cherry

INSTRUCTIONS

1. Pre-heat the oven to 180°C/160°C fan.
2. Using a knob of butter, grease a 23cm tart tin.
3. Roll out the ready-made shortcrust pastry on a floured surface until it is the same size as your tart tin. Place inside the tin and trim off any overlapping edges with a sharp knife.
4. Bake the pastry case blind for 15 minutes by putting greaseproof paper into the case, over the pastry and weighing it down with baking beans. Once baked, remove the paper and beans and leave to the side whist you make your filling.

TIP: If you haven't got baking beans you can easily use rice. It is just to prevent the base of the case from rising during baking.

5. Beat together the sugar and butter until light and fluffy, then add the eggs and give a good stir.
6. Add the flour then the almond extract and make sure everything is mixed together fully.
7. Spread the jam on top of the pastry then add your almond mixture on top. Make sure the pastry case has cooled before this step to ensure that the jam does not melt into the pastry case.
8. Return to the oven and bake for a further 20 minutes. Then leave to cool before removing from the tin.
9. Add 2-3 tablespoons of water to the icing sugar and give it a good stir until you achieve a thick mixture. Swirl the icing on top of your Bakewell tart then finish off with a glacé cherry in the middle.

TIP: It is not essential to use cherry jam with this recipe. You can easily experiment with other jams such as strawberry and raspberry, which tend to be more readily available at home and equally as delicious.

AFTERNOON TEA

DAIRY MILK FUDGE

I love this recipe! Having a recipe for fudge that is so easy to make and tastes absolutely delicious is a wonderful thing to have in your back pocket for any time, but especially for an afternoon tea. I use this treat in my Cadbury's afternoon tea. This recipe can also be adapted with any of your favourite chocolates. You can use milk chocolate instead of the white chocolate which I have used in this recipe. It is a very sweet, rich recipe and you only need a small piece to get that ultimate fudge craving. It also makes a great present for someone who needs a sweet pick-me-up! No boiling or sugar thermometers, just quick and easy fudge...

Serves 12

Preparation time 15 minutes

Chilling time 3 hours

Will keep in the fridge for at least 2 weeks

You'll need:

Large mixing bowl

Heatproof bowl

Large metal spoon

9 inch x 9 inch baking tin

Greaseproof paper

INGREDIENTS

397 g condensed milk

400 g white chocolate

Bar of 110g Cadbury's Dairy Milk

INSTRUCTIONS

1. Line a 9 x 9 inch tin with greaseproof paper.
2. Chop the chocolate into a microwaveable bowl and melt in the microwave for 1 minute bursts until all the chocolate has melted.
3. Pour the condensed milk into the chocolate and give a good stir. It will start to thicken really quickly so keep with it until you get a lovely thick fudge mixture.
4. Pour the fudge into your tin and smooth the mixture out so you get an even layer, then add the Dairy Milk chunks.
5. Place in the fridge for about 3 hours till set.

Tip: You can use milk, white or dark chocolate and any chocolates of your choice, and even a drizzle of Carnation caramel or any supermarket's own chocolate drizzle.

OCCASIONS

It's tradition to celebrate birthdays, Christmas and Easter with a celebration cake or treats. I always think it builds strong relationships between generations celebrating any occasion, especially children, who will always remember these special experiences. Preparing a celebration treat for that special someone shows how much you care.

Each of my treats represent a special occasion and most of them are so easy to do and easy to prepare ahead. As well as birthdays, Easter and Christmas, I have popped in some recipes for Valentine's Day and Halloween or Bonfire night.

Take any opportunity to celebrate things we are blessed with.

Because it is a special time of year, I have cheated a bit and you may find a few ingredients which aren't in your store cupboard essentials. However, as always, I have given you alternatives where possible.

BIRTHDAY

A birthday cake is an essential when it comes to celebrations. It adds more happiness to the occasion and makes a perfect gift. Plus, it is definitely an excuse to eat cake – like you need an excuse! In this section, there are also alternatives to cake, as not everyone likes a birthday cake or sponge cake, so I have added some yummy birthday doughnuts and some alternative treats for the chocolate lovers. I have you covered for all birthday treats for your loved ones.

VALENTINE'S DAY

Valentine's day is the perfect time to show your partner how much they mean to you and how much you care. I always think that taking that little extra time out of your daily routine and baking homemade treats for the one you love rather than giving shop bought just shows you have gone that extra mile. Plus, if you are anything like our household, we celebrate Valentine's day as a whole family and I always bake my kids treats too and make them feel involved. This has been something passed down to me as my lovely mum and dad always made a fuss of me and my brother around Valentine's day.

EASTER

This time of year has got to be one of my favourite times to try new and different treats. Let's face it, we all let ourselves go and enjoy the Easter celebrations! As a bonus, it's the time of year I can get hold of Creme eggs and Mini eggs to use in all my recipes – yes!

HALLOWEEN AND BONFIRE NIGHT

I love this time of year – cosy nights in with a cup of hot chocolate and your favourite sweet treat. And it's the time of the year when my Cinder Toffee is baked – a traditional British treat loved by children and grown-ups. These treats are perfect for Halloween and bonfire night treats, whether you're having a family bonfire night party or simply making them to hand out to those trick or treaters.

CHRISTMAS

Christmas treats make the season so magical. We always bake together as a family this time of year, especially me with my little girl, and make our favourite treats for our Christmas Eve buffet. ? Plus this time of year, we forget about those diets for once and enjoy all our favourite things!

OCCASIONS: BIRTHDAY

BIRTHDAY BROWNIE CAKE

This moist and tender cake is a winner in my household and is for the brownie lovers out there. I make this cake a lot for birthday celebrations for my customers as its slightly different to your normal sponge cake. It is made using real blocks of chocolate; the ingredients I use are exactly the same as my brownie traybakes but I've added a few extras. You can add any of your favourite chocolates, but I have used Kinder Bueno in this recipe with a chocolate buttercream.

Serves 12

Preparation time 15 minutes
Baking time 40 minutes
Cool time 1 hour
Keeps in an airtight container for up to 6 days

You'll need:

Large mixing bowl
Heatproof bowl
Large metal spoon
Scales
Two 8 inch round baking tins
Greaseproof paper

INGREDIENTS

345 g butter
450 g caster sugar
210 g flour
9 eggs
3 tablespoons of cocoa powder
300 g dark chocolate (supermarket's own is fine)

Buttercream

200 g butter
400 g icing sugar
30 g cocoa powder

INSTRUCTIONS

1. Pre-heat your oven to 180°C/160° fan.

2. Grease two 8 inch cake tins with butter and line them with greaseproof paper.

3. Place the butter and chocolate in a heatproof bowl and microwave in 60 second bursts till all the chocolate has melted. Leave to the side to cool slightly.

4. Place the eggs and caster sugar into a bowl and give a good stir. Once the chocolate has cooled slightly and it's easy to handle the bowl, pour the mixture into the eggs mixture and give another good stir.

5. Add the flour and cocoa powder to the bowl and then finally give all your ingredients a good stir until everything is evenly distributed. Pour the mixture evenly into the two cake tins and bake for about 50 minutes. You will know it is baked when a knife comes out clean when inserted into the cake. Let the cakes cool whilst you prepare your buttercream.

6. Mix the butter and icing sugar in a bowl then slowly add the cocoa powder. If you find the buttercream is a little thick to spread, add a couple of tablespoons of milk.

7. Spread the buttercream on one side of your cake then sandwich the two cakes together. Use the rest of your buttercream on top then add any of your favourite chocolates. I use Kinder Bueno and Kinder chocolate bars for this cake.

TIP: This brownie cake keeps moist much longer than a sponge cake. That makes it ideal if your only time to bake is a few days before that special birthday. Just keep it in an airtight container and you can keep going at this yummy cake for up to 6 days – if it lasts that long in your house!

OCCASIONS: BIRTHDAY

BROWNIE CHOCOLATE DOUGHNUTS

These yummy doughnuts are super easy to whip up, and great for any birthday celebration. Think about it – you can have fresh doughnuts in less than 20 minutes and you can decorate them with any of your favourite chocolate toppings. ☺ These doughnuts are also much healthier than the fried ones so you won't get that guilty feeling when biting into one. You can even have these doughnuts left uncovered without chocolate and they still give that yummy fulfilment. I mean, is there anything better than a warm yummy doughnut? ☺

Serves 6 doughnuts
Preparation time 10 minutes
Baking time 20 minutes
Will keep in an airtight container for 2 days

You'll need:
Large mixing bowl
Heatproof bowl
Large metal spoon
Scales
6-hole doughnut tin

INGREDIENTS

120 g self raising flour
70 g caster sugar
30 g butter
1 egg
100 ml full fat or semi skimmed milk
6-hole doughnut muffin tray

INSTRUCTIONS

1. Preheat your oven to 180 °C/160° fan.

2. In a large bowl, mix together the caster sugar and eggs, then add the butter and flour until everything is incorporated.

3. Add the milk to the doughnut batter and give a final good stir until no flour bits remain, but try not to overmix, to make sure that the sponge is light and fluffy.

4. Now pour your batter into the doughnut cavities. I just use a measuring jug to do this as its simply the easiest and quickest way to cover each doughnut mould.

5. Place the mould into the oven and bake for 20 minutes.

6. Remove from the oven and let the doughnuts cool in the pan. Whilst they are cooling you can leave them how they are. If you want a little extra, you can decorate them with any of your favourite chocolate by melting the chocolate in a microwaveable safe bowl and drizzling on top of your doughnuts.

7. Let the chocolate set on the doughnuts by either chilling in the fridge or leaving in a cool area.

Tip: Turn these yummy doughnuts into cupcakes instead by using a 12-hole cupcake tin and using cupcake cases.

OCCASIONS: BIRTHDAY

BIRTHDAY CHOCOLATE LOLLIPOPS

These gorgeous chocolate lollipops are just perfect for your little one's birthdays and great for birthday parties too as a gift for your children's friends to take home. I use chocolate moulds for my customers but I have done this recipe without, so that no chocolate moulds are necessary. These lollipops are also great as a gift for any birthday or Christmas too, and the best part is that they are absolutely so easy to do and can be stored in the fridge for a good while as no fresh dairy products are included, simply chocolate. ☺

Makes 4 lollipops

Preparation time 10 minutes

No baking required

Chilling time in the fridge 1 hour to set

You'll need:

Large mixing bowl

Heatproof bowl

Large metal spoon

Greaseproof paper

INGREDIENTS

200 g milk chocolate, dark chocolate or white chocolate

Multi-coloured sprinkles

A box of Smarties or any of your favourite toppings

4 lollipop sticks or you can even use straws

TIP: You can also use white chocolate and add a couple of drops of food colouring to make different coloured lollipops. Why not even treat your trick or treaters and decorate them with Halloween edible treats too. Basically, they are great for any occasion! ☺

INSTRUCTIONS

1. Line a baking tin with greaseproof paper.
2. Break the chocolate into pieces and place in a microwaveable safe bowl. Melt the chocolate in 30 second bursts until all the chocolate is fully melted.
3. Place tablespoons of the chocolate onto the greaseproof paper, then insert the lollipop stick or straw a third of the way into the chocolate until about three quarters to the top of the blob of chocolate.
4. Decorate with your sprinkles and your favourite chocolates and place in the fridge to cool completely.

Tip: For an adult's version, use the same method as above but substitute with your favourite chocolate. Why not add any your favourite fruits? For a different yummy flavour, add half/half of chocolate and cream cheese and a sprinkle of crushed digestive biscuits for a lovely cheesecake lollipop.

OCCASIONS: BIRTHDAY

TERRY'S CHOCOLATE ORANGE ICE-CREAM

This is such a super easy ice cream to make. I use the base of this recipe in all my flavoured ice creams. This is also my favourite flavour. I absolutely love Terry's chocolate orange and you get a real depth of flavour with the orange in this ice cream. There is no churning involved so it is super quick to make too. This ice cream will go delicious with my Kinder Bueno birthday cake or, let's face it, with any yummy desert. It can be made ahead for that special birthday occasion. All you need to do is take it out of the freezer and let it defrost slightly before serving and most of all, enjoy!

Serves 4
Preparation time 15 minutes
Freezing time 6 hours
Thaw time 30 minutes

You'll need:
Large mixing bowl
Hand mixer
Large metal spoon
Freezer-proof container

INGREDIENTS

600 ml double cream
397 g tin of condensed milk
300 g Terry's chocolate orange

INSTRUCTIONS

1. Chop three quarters of the Terry's chocolate orange pieces and place into a microwave safe bowl. Melt in 30 second bursts until fully melted, then put to the side.

2. Pour the cream into a mixing bowl and whisk until it is the texture of a thick mousse, then add the condensed milk and melted chocolate. Give the mixture a final whisk for a minute until it holds itself.

3. Spoon the ice cream into a freezer-proof container and top with the remaining Terry's chocolate orange segments.

4. Freeze for 6 hours. When you want to serve, ideally take it out of the freezer 30 minutes beforehand.

TIP: You can change the flavour of this ice cream by replacing the Terry's chocolate orange with any of your favourite chocolates or even biscuits. Another delicious flavour is Oreo ice cream. Rather than melting chocolate, just whisk the double cream and condensed milk then add a packet of crushed Oreos. Or you could try my popular mint chocolate chip. Again, same ingredients but adding a teaspoon of mint extract and a packet of chocolate chips.

OCCASIONS: BIRTHDAY

SWEET BURGER AND CHIPS

These sweet treats are great for any birthday or party and ideal for both kids and adults. The 'burger' is made from a homemade brownie, the 'chips' are made from vanilla shortbread, and the 'buns' from vanilla sponge cakes. They will surprise your guests when they have seen what you have created. You will have lots of fun making these sweet treats with your young ones – building the different parts together once they have been cooked is the fun part

Serves 6

Preparation time 60 minutes

Baking time 25-35 minutes each bake

Will keep in an airtight container for 2 to 3 days

You'll need:

Large mixing bowl
Heatproof bowl
Large metal spoon
Scales
9 inch x 9 inch baking tin
12 inch x 8 inch baking tin
12-hole cupcake tin
Greaseproof paper

INGREDIENTS

For the burger (Brownie)
115 g butter
100 g dark chocolate
150 g caster sugar
3 eggs
70 g plain flour
2 tablespoons of cocoa powder

For the shortbread (Fries)
345 g plain flour
150 g caster sugar
227 g butter
100g green fondant icing
4 strawberries

For the cupcakes (Buns)
120 g butter
120 g sugar
2 eggs
120 g self-raising flour
Sprinkle of desiccated coconut

INSTRUCTIONS

For the brownies

1. Preheat the oven to 180°C/160°C fan and line a baking tin with greaseproof paper.
2. Melt together 100 g of the dark chocolate and butter in a heatproof (and microwaveable) dish in the microwave for about 1 minute and then set aside to cool.
3. Using an electric whisk or hand whisk, stir the eggs with the caster sugar until light and fluffy.
4. Pour the chocolate and butter mixture into the caster sugar and eggs and give it a good stir to make sure everything's incorporated together.
5. Sift the flour and cocoa powder into the brownie mixture and give it a good stir. Make sure you don't overmix as you don't want to knock any air out of the brownie mixture, but make sure everything's mixed together. Put your gooey brownie mixture into a 12 inch x 9 inch baking tin.

OCCASIONS: BIRTHDAY

6. Bake in the oven for approximately 25 minutes but make sure you don't over bake as you want that slightly gooey mixture in the inside but still making sure its cooked. Don't forget the visual and toothpick tests.

7. Leave to the side to cool and then using a round cookie cutter (or a mug), cut out 6 circles in the shape of a burger.

For the buns
1. Preheat your oven to 200°C/180°C fan.

2. Line a 12-hole muffin tin with cupcake cases, and beat together the sugar and eggs until creamy. Then add the butter and flour and give a good stir until all the ingredients are incorporated.

3. Fill your cupcake cases three quarters full and bake in the oven for approximately 20-25 minutes. Leave to the side to cool. Once cooled, slice the end of each cake to make a neat edge.

> **TIP: To finish off the cupcake I use desiccated coconut to look like seeds**

For the fries
1. Preheat your oven to 200°C/180°C fan.

2. Combine the flour and sugar in a large bowl, then add the butter. Using your fingertips or a large spoon, mix the ingredients together until you get a lovely dough texture.

3. Grease a 9 x 9 inch tin with greaseproof paper and add your dough. Make sure the whole tin is covered in an even layer.

4. Bake the shortbread for 30-35 minutes until it is a light brown colour.

5. Leave to cool in the tin at the side. Once cooled, cut into strips about 1 inch wide to make into fries.

> To assemble the burger, place a 'bun' cupcake on a plate followed by your 'burger' brownie, then place another 'bun' cupcake on top. I decorated the burgers by using green fondant icing for the lettuce, cutting small slices and putting on top of the brownie, and a fresh strawberry cut in half to look like a tomato.

OCCASIONS: VALENTINE'S DAY

ROSE CUPCAKE BOUQUET

This cupcake bouquet is one of my most popular products for Valentine's, and Mother's day too. It's such a lovely gift to send to a loved one and has the wow effect. They are so easy to make, with a simple cupcake recipe which can be vanilla or choc sponge, decorated with your loved one's favourite toppings. You can buy cupcake bouquet holders from any cake store online – and there's so many colours to choose from too.

Makes 7 cupcakes

Preparation time 20 minutes

Baking time 40 minutes

Will keep in an airtight container for 4 days

You'll need:

Large mixing bowl

Heatproof bowl

Large metal spoon

Scales

12-hole cupcake tin

Cupcake bouquet holder (or arrange them on a plate or board to look like a bouquet)

INGREDIENTS

120 g butter

120 g caster sugar

120 g self-raising flour

2 eggs

For the buttercream icing

140 g butter

275 g icing sugar

1-2 tablespoons of milk

TIP: You can easily make these yummy cakes into a chocolate cupcake by adding 30 g cocoa powder in at the start when adding the flour.

INSTRUCTIONS

1. Preheat oven to 180°C/160°C fan and line a baking tin with 7 cupcake cases.
2. Mix the butter and sugar in a bowl then beat in the eggs and give another a good stir until fully incorporated.
3. Fold in the flour then add the milk. Spoon the mixture into your cupcake cases until they are three quarters full.
4. Bake in the oven for approximately 15-20 minutes, then set aside to cool whilst you make your buttercream.
5. For the buttercream, beat the butter until softened, then gradually add the icing sugar a little at a time until it's all used up. Add a little milk if it starts to thicken too much until it's a creamy consistency.
6. Spoon the buttercream over your cupcakes.

TIP: You can also decorate these cupcakes with lots of different chocolate toppings or sweets or fresh fruit and colourful sprinkles.

OCCASIONS: VALENTINE'S DAY

RED VELVET COOKIES

Red velvet is a mixture of chocolate and vanilla. The red comes from food colouring. It's a delicious chunky cookie with white chocolate chips which look absolutely fabulous against the red cookie. These are great for any parties or special occasions and especially for Valentine's day. Your loved one will thank you when they receive these yummy treats. Who doesn't like a cookie? You could also use these cookies for an afternoon tea spread, but I think personally they are definitely a winner in my eyes for Valentine's Day.

Makes 6 large cookies

Preparation time 15 minutes

Baking time 20 minutes

Keeps in an airtight container for 4 to 5 days

You'll need:

Large mixing bowl

Heatproof bowl

Large metal spoon

Scales

Baking tin

Greaseproof paper

INGREDIENTS

150 g melted butter

150 g sugar

1 egg

150 g plain flour

85 g white chocolate chips

2 teaspoons of red food colouring

INSTRUCTIONS

1. Preheat your oven to 180°C/160°C fan and line a large flat baking tin with greaseproof paper.

2. Beat the eggs and sugar until nice and creamy then add the melted butter and incorporate everything by stirring.

3. Add the flour followed by the chocolate chips until you form a cookie dough texture, then finally add the red food colouring. If you find the dough is a little bit runny, add a little bit more flour until the dough holds itself slightly.

4. Roll 6 large cookie dough balls of equal size. Place them on your tin and bake in the oven for around 20 minutes. The cookies bake further on the tin after taking them out of the oven so if they do feel a little soft, that's fine as they will harden slightly after being baked.

Tip: You could decorate the top of the cookies with heart sprinkles or edible glitter. The shops have lots of lovely themed cake decorations this time of year in the baking aisles.

OCCASIONS: EASTER

CREME EGG LOAF

Creme eggs are an absolute must for an Easter bake. They are such a classic treat and go so well with this chocolate loaf cake. The only Creme eggs in this cake are decorations on the top, as I prefer a light chocolate sponge loaf for this recipe. However, you could add Creme eggs into the sponge too if you like your cake very gooey. All you do is put half the mixture into the tin, then a line of three Creme eggs halved, then add the rest of the mixture. You can also adapt this loaf cake and add mini eggs, or any of your favourite chocolates to the top of the loaf.

Serves 6

Preparation time 15 minutes

Baking time 40 minutes

Will keep in an airtight container for 4 days

You'll need:

Large mixing bowl

Heatproof bowl

Large metal spoon

Scales

Loaf tin

Greaseproof paper

INGREDIENTS

250 g butter

250 g caster sugar

200 g self raising flour

50 g cocoa powder

5 eggs

Pack of 5 Creme eggs

100 g melted white chocolate

INSTRUCTIONS

1. Preheat your oven to 180°C/160°C fan and grease and line a loaf tin with greaseproof paper.
2. Beat the sugar and eggs together until light and fluffy then add in the butter and give another good stir.
3. Add in your flour and cocoa powder and beat again till smooth.
4. Pour into the tin and bake for 40 minutes or until baked through (a knife comes out clean when put in the top).
5. Leave the cake to cool fully before drizzling with white chocolate, then finish off by topping with Creme eggs cut in half.

Tip: Instead of using Creme eggs, try another type of chocolate. If you are anything like our household, with two children we get lots of Easter eggs delivered by our lovely family members. You could decorate the top with broken up Easter egg shells or any spare chocolates from inside them – looks really indulgent too! Yesssss!

OCCASIONS: EASTER

MINI EGG CHOCOLATE CAKE

This is a perfect Easter showstopper – a two-layer chocolate sponge cake filled and topped with vanilla buttercream and finished off with whole and crushed mini eggs. It also looks really pretty and certainly looks fabulous in the middle of your Easter table. Just like my other Easter recipes, you can use any of your other favourite chocolates too – Creme eggs or smarties, whatever you prefer.

Serves 12

Preparation time 20 minutes
Baking time 40 minutes
Will keep in an airtight container for 4 days

You'll need:

Large mixing bowl
Heatproof bowl
Large metal spoon
Scales
Two 8 inch round cake tins
Greaseproof paper

INGREDIENTS

400 g butter (melted)
400 g caster sugar
400 g self-raising flour
50 g cocoa powder
7 eggs

For the buttercream
350 g salted butter
700 g icing sugar
Large bag of mini eggs

Tip: You can make this a plain vanilla sponge by simply leaving the cocoa powder out of the recipe.

INSTRUCTIONS

1. Preheat your oven to 180°C/160°C fan and line and grease two 8-inch baking tins with greaseproof paper.

2. Beat together the eggs and caster sugar until light and fluffy and add the melted butter and give another good stir until everything's incorporated.

3. Add the cocoa powder and give another good mix, then divide the batter between the cake tins. Bake in the oven for approximately 40 minutes, until a knife inserted into the cakes come out clean.

4. Take the cake out of the tin and set aside, leaving it to cool completely whilst you make your buttercream.

5. In a large bowl, add the icing sugar to the butter and give a good stir for about 5 minutes until it forms a really thick consistency and yet is fluffy.

6. Spread half of the buttercream on one side of one of the cakes and then sandwich the two cakes together. Use the rest of the buttercream on top of the cake.

7. Decorate your Easter cake with mini eggs however you wish. You can even use colourful sprinkles if you have any spare in your cupboard.

65

OCCASIONS: EASTER

MINI EGG TOPPED MERINGUES

I love how cute these meringues look. I also love anything meringue! I find them so fresh and tasty that I just want more and more. If you have not made meringue before it can seem a bit daunting, but honestly, it's really quite easy to do as long as you have a clean bowl and whisk, with no egg yolk. You can't go wrong. I use this meringue recipe for an extra-large fruit pavlova as well, but instead of dividing the mixture into small dollops, I just separate the mixture in two. You can also add buttercream or whipping cream on top, whatever you prefer.

Serves 8

Preparation time 20 minutes
Baking time 40 minutes
Will keep in the fridge for 2 days

You'll need:

Large mixing bowl
Heatproof bowl
Large metal spoon
Baking tin
Hand mixer
Greaseproof paper

INGREDIENTS

7 egg whites
225 g caster sugar
1 teaspoon of white wine vinegar
1 teaspoon of cornflour
450 ml double cream
2 tablespoons of sugar
Pack of mini eggs

TIP: You can use buttercream instead of double cream for this recipe, or why not even melt 100g milk chocolate and mix it with the whipped cream. Plus, you can add any of your favourite chocolate toppings instead.

INSTRUCTIONS

1. Preheat your oven to 120°C/100°C fan and line two large tins with greaseproof paper, then leave to the side.

2. Making sure your bowl and hand whisk are thoroughly clean, add in your egg whites and whip them up to stiff peaks. This should take approximately a good 10 minutes until the egg whites have doubled in size. This is a brilliant workout for your arms!

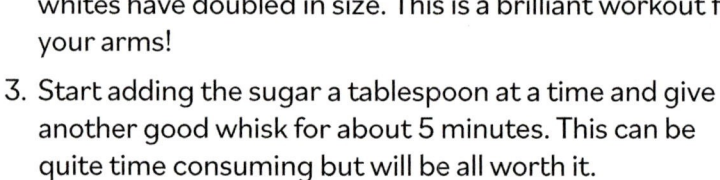

3. Start adding the sugar a tablespoon at a time and give another good whisk for about 5 minutes. This can be quite time consuming but will be all worth it.

4. Once all the sugar has been mixed, add in the white wine vinegar and flour and whisk again for about 2 minutes. To make sure it's the right consistency, place the bowl over your head and if it's right, no mixture will tip. ☺

5. Dollop a large spoonful of meringue onto the tins. You should get approximately 8 meringues altogether. Bake in the oven for about 40-50 minutes.

6. Once baked, switch the oven off and leave the tins in the oven to cool for about 50 minutes.

7. Whip the double cream and sugar together till you form soft peaks and dollop onto your cooled meringue. Finally, decorate with the mini eggs.

OCCASIONS: HALLOWEEN AND BONFIRE NIGHT

STICKY TOFFEE APPLE CAKE

Sticky Toffee Pudding in a cake – need we say more? ☺ This cake is a traditional British desert and has been around for many years. I have made it a modern twist with the toffee apples on top. This cake is an ultimate classic. It's the perfect cake for a Bonfire night gathering. I love the rich flavour, with black treacle and the hint of cinnamon. You can serve it warm or as it is, with either custard, cream or ice cream, whichever your favourite. ☺

Serves 12
Preparation time 15 minutes
Baking time 40 minutes
Cool time 1 hour
Keeps in an airtight container for 4-5 days

You'll need:
Large mixing bowl
Heatproof bowl
Large metal spoon
Scales
Two 8 inch round cake tins
Greaseproof paper

INGREDIENTS

125 g butter
225 g caster sugar
180 ml boiling water
250 g self raising flour
4 eggs
60 g black treacle or golden syrup
2 tablespoons of cinnamon

Buttercream
200 g butter
400 g icing sugar

3 red sticky toffee apples

INSTRUCTIONS

1. Preheat your oven to 180°C/160°C fan and line two 8-inch cake tins with greaseproof paper.

2. Place the butter and sugar in a large bowl and beat until it turns into a lovely creamy texture.

3. Add the eggs, water and flour and give another good stir until everything has combined, then finally add the black treacle and cinnamon and stir it in.

4. Pour the mixture into the tins and bake in the oven for approximately 40 minutes until a knife inserted into the cake comes out clean (just insert slightly without taking the cake out of the tin).

5. Leave to cool in the tin for an hour whilst you make your buttercream.

6. To make the buttercream, tip the icing sugar and butter into a bowl and give it a good mix. If the mixture feels a little too thick, add a little bit of milk.

7. Spread half of the mixture on one side of the cakes and sandwich together, then top with the rest of the buttercream and then decorate with your sticky toffee apples.

Tip: You can easily make your own cinder toffee apples to use as decoration by using my cinder toffee recipe, which is my next recipe. As soon as you have made the cinder toffee, cover your apples carefully and try not to spill any of the syrup. Leave to the side and let the delicious cinder toffee set on the apples.

OCCASIONS: HALLOWEEN AND BONFIRE NIGHT

MILK CHOC CINDER TOFFEE

Cinder Toffee is something we traditionally eat on Bonfire night, but you can also eat this yummy treat all year round. It's absolutely delicious covered in milk chocolate. This recipe is a favourite for the Cadbury's Crunchie lovers, but this recipe makes amazing bigger chunky pieces, so even better, right? ☺ A wonderful treat around the fire with friends and family.

Serves 4

Preparation time 15 minutes

Cool time 1 hour in the fridge

Keeps in an airtight container for 7 days

You'll need:

Saucepan

Large metal spoon

Scales

9 inch x 9 inch baking tin

Greaseproof paper

INGREDIENTS

200 g caster sugar

4 tablespoons of golden syrup

1 tablespoon of bicarbonate of soda

200 g melted milk chocolate

INSTRUCTIONS

1. Prepare a 9 x 9 inch baking tin with greaseproof paper.

2. In a large pan, add the sugar and syrup on a medium heat and give a good stir until the sugar starts to melt.

3. Keep stirring to make sure the ingredients doesn't stick to the pan. It should start to have a runny texture and to go a lovely golden colour. Don't overcook the mixture. It should take about 5 minutes to start to go runny.

4. Remove the pan from the heat and immediately add the baking soda. Quickly mix the ingredients together. You will notice that the mixture will start to bubble. As soon as it does, pour into the tin. Be very careful there are no spillages as this mixture is extremely hot and could burn your skin.

5. Let the mixture set for about 30 minutes. As you wait, put the chocolate into a microwaveable dish and cook in 20 second bursts till all the chocolate has melted.

6. Once the mixture has cooled, pour the melted chocolate over it.

7. Put in the fridge to set for about an hour. Then break into pieces – as big as you dare!

Tip: You could even make little gifts for your loved ones by breaking the cinder toffee into small chunks, putting them in a small gift bag tied with a bow. ☺

OCCASIONS: HALLOWEEN AND BONFIRE NIGHT

SMORES BROWNIES

These Brownies are absolutely delicious. A gooey brownie topped with crackers, marshmallows and chocolate chips, perfect for any party or especially bonfire night. The brownie method is exactly the same as my previous brownie recipes. The only thing you're changing is the topping, so rather than covering with chocolate, you are creating that yummy smores treat for that extra indulgence. These are enjoyable for both children and adults, and you will certainly have empty plates and no crumbs! ☺

Makes 6 pieces
Preparation 20 minutes
Bake 20 minutes
Cool 1 hour
Lasts 5-6 days at room temperature when stored in an airtight container.

You'll need:
Large mixing bowl
Heatproof bowl
Large metal spoon
Scales
12 inch x 8 inch baking tin
Greaseproof paper

INGREDIENTS

For the brownie
150 g caster sugar
200 g dark chocolate
115 g butter (salted or unsalted)
3 small eggs
50 g cocoa powder

For the Smores
10 cream crackers crushed
150 g bag mini marshmallows
Pack of chocolate chips

INSTRUCTIONS

1. Preheat the oven to 180°C/160°C fan and line a baking tin with greaseproof paper.
2. Melt together 100 g of the dark chocolate and butter in a heatproof dish in the microwave for about 1 minute and then set aside to cool.
3. Using an electric whisk or spoon, whisk the eggs with the caster sugar until light and fluffy.
4. Pour the chocolate and butter mixture into the caster sugar and eggs and give it a good stir. Make sure everything's incorporated together.
5. Sift the flour and cocoa powder into the brownie mixture and give it a good stir. Make sure you don't overmix as you don't want to knock any air out of the brownie mixture but make sure everything's mixed together. Bake in the oven for about 20 minutes,
6. 5 minutes before the brownies finish cooking, add your marshmallows, crackers and chocolate chips and place back in the oven for a further 5 minutes.
7. Chill at the side for about an hour before cutting into 6 large pieces.

Tip: Use this Smores recipe to bake delicious cookies instead. The recipe should make about 6 cookies. Simply use 150g caster sugar, 115g butter, 150g flour and 1 egg. Place about 6 cookie-sized dollops of the mixture on a baking tin and bake in the oven at the same temperature for 20 minutes. 5 minutes before the end of the cooking time, add the crackers, marshmallows and chocolate chips then put them back in the oven for a further 5 minutes.

OCCASIONS: CHRISTMAS

CHRISTMAS TREE MINCE PIE

Let me show you the most incredible showstopping festive desert. For the mince pie lovers and with just three ingredients, this Christmas Tree Mince Pie is so easy to create. You can also adapt this recipe by changing the filling, so rather than using mincemeat you could use Nutella, Biscoff spread, or even tinned cherries. This is a great festive treat to go in the centre of your table so everyone can tuck in and enjoy a slice.

Serves 12

Preparation time 15 minutes
Baking time 25 minutes
Cool time 10 minutes
This will keep in an airtight container for 3 days

You'll need:

Large mixing bowl
Large metal spoon
Scales
Baking tin
Greaseproof paper

INGREDIENTS

2 sheets of pre rolled puff pastry
100 g mince meat
1 egg
2 tablespoons of icing sugar

INSTRUCTIONS

1. Preheat your oven to 180°C/160°C fan and line a baking sheet with greaseproof paper.
2. Unroll one of your sheets of puff pastry and put it on your baking sheet.
3. Spread the mincemeat onto the pastry, making sure the whole of the pastry is covered. Unroll the second puff pastry sheet and place on top of the mincemeat.
4. Cut the pastry into the shape of a Christmas tree with a knife, and remove the excess pastry from around your Christmas tree.
5. Beat the egg and, using an old unused paintbrush, or even you fingers, brush the egg over the tree.
6. Bake the Christmas tree for approximately 20-35 minutes until starts to go a golden brown. Transfer to a serving board and dust with icing sugar.

TIP: It can even be made ahead and frozen ready for the big day. After shaping the tree, wrap it in greaseproof paper and it can be put in the freezer. When you take it out, allow it to defrost (should take 3-4 hours) and then brush with the egg wash and bake.

OCCASIONS: CHRISTMAS

CHRISTMAS GINGERBREAD CAKE

This is such a delicious cake and so Christmassy. With its treacle base, it has all the Christmas feels. I love the flavour of the ginger and the smell in the kitchen when it is baking is absolutely divine. It's a simple vanilla frosting with lots of gingerbread men on top to give that festive look. You can also keep this plain and simple by using just vanilla buttercream on top of the cake. You will get so many compliments on how moist this cake is too, and such a rich flavour.

Serves 12
Preparation time 20 minutes
Baking time 40 minutes
Cool time 1 hour
This cake will keep in an airtight container for at least 3-4 days

You'll need:
Large mixing bowl
Heatproof bowl
Large metal spoon
Scales
8 inch round cake tin
Greaseproof paper

INGREDIENTS
250 g butter
250 g caster sugar
250 g golden syrup
250 g black treacle (this can be done without if you don't have it in your cupboard)
500 g self raising flour
4 tablespoons of ground ginger
3 eggs
350 ml whole milk

Tip: You could add stem ginger on top instead for a more adult feel.

Frosting
250 g butter
500 g icing sugar
Mini gingerbread men for decoration

INSTRUCTIONS

1. Pre Heat your oven to 180°C/160°C fan. Grease and line two 8-inch round baking tins.

2. Add the butter and eggs to a bowl and give a good stir, then add the butter followed by the golden syrup and black treacle (but this isn't essential if you don't have black treacle in your store cupboard – I have tried this recipe with and without and it is just as yummy. With a large spoon, stir thoroughly for a couple of minutes until everything's incorporated together.

3. Sift the flour into the bowl with the ground ginger and finally add the milk. Give a final good stir.

4. Split the mixture between the two tins and bake in the oven for 40 to 50 minutes. You know when the cake is baked thoroughly if you insert a knife into the cake and it comes out clean. Leave the cakes to the side in their tins to cool completely.

5. To make your frosting, beat the butter and icing sugar together. I simply use a metal spoon to do this. Spread the buttercream on one side of the cake and then sandwich them together. Finish the top of the cake with the rest of the buttercream.

6. Add your gingerbread man around the cake if using.

OCCASIONS: CHRISTMAS

CHRISTMAS FRUIT CAKE

Christmas cake is a traditional fruit cake with a rich yummy texture. This cake doesn't need to be made months in advanced like a lot of fruit cakes. It is so easy to prepare too and keeps for ages. This is made without alcohol so great for everyone. ☺ It is one of my husband's favourite cakes; he loves anything with fruit and sponge. This cake can be baked at any time of year, not just the festive season, but there is just something about the traditional fruit cake that just shouts out Christmas. This cake can also be made in advanced and stored if you want to be ahead of yourself over the festive period. There are a few non essential ingredients here, but with it being Christmas, a few extras for this special season can be added on this occasion.

Serves 12

Preparation time 20 minutes

Baking time 1 hour

Cool time 1 hour

Keeps in an airtight container for a couple of weeks

You'll need:

Large mixing bowl

Heatproof bowl

Large metal spoon

Scales

8 inch round cake tin

Greaseproof paper

INGREDIENTS

150 g glacé cherries

250 g sultanas

250 g raisins

250 g butter

250 g sugar

200 g plain flour

4 eggs

1 teaspoon of cinnamon

1 teaspoon of ground ginger

1 teaspoon of mixed spice

1 tablespoon of treacle

INSTRUCTIONS

1. Pre-heat your oven to 180°C/160°C fan and grease and line two 8 inch baking tins with greaseproof paper.

2. Cream together the butter and sugar until light and fluffy, then add the eggs and mix well after each adding each one.

3. Add the treacle then the flour and give a good stir until everything's incorporated together. Fold in the fruit with the spices and give another final stirring.

4. Pour into the two tins and level with a spoon. Bake in the oven for about 1 hour until a knife inserted in the cake comes out clean.

TIP: You can decorate your Christmas cake however you fancy. I like to cover mine with apricot jam then ready rolled marzipan and white fondant icing, but you could leave it bare and put some pretty fake holly on top, drizzle some icing on top, or even sprinkle it with edible glitter!

A NOTE FROM NICKY

So there you go, all of my recipes in one book for you to have a good old go at – well, a lot of them, at least, because I'm always inventing new ones, so by the time this book comes out, I'll have loads more to share! I hope you enjoy baking them as much as I do every day in my baking room for my lovely customers.

I do find baking so therapeutic and it helps me so much with my mental health too, which has been a huge part of my life since I was a teenager. As soon as my apron is on, I am in relaxation mode.

When I'm not baking, I am always researching new treats to create. I have just recently opened my own pop up shop at home, which has been a huge success and it has been lovely to see all my customers and have a chat – something I'm rather good at, talking.

I would love to see any creations you have made from my recipes, so please feel free to contact me on Nickycain@me.com. I am also on Facebook as Nicky Cains and Instagram too: nickycainsbrownies.

Happy baking!

Nicky X

Enjoy!

Printed in Great Britain
by Amazon